The
New Locust Years

Trouble in the Woods & the destruction of ancient woodland heritage in the UK

Ian D. Rotherham

The New Locust Years:
Trouble in the Woods & the destruction of ancient woodland heritage in the UK

Ian D. Rotherham

ISBN: 978-1-904098-76-8

Published by: Wildtrack Publishing, Ash Tree Yard, 62-68 Thirlwell Rd, Heeley, Sheffield, S8 9TF

Typeset and processed by Christine Handley & Ian D. Rotherham

Contents

Whinacre Wood, Moss Valley, Derbyshire

Ancient linear feature and monument, Iron Age or Dark Ages, Whitwell Wood, Derbyshire

Foreword & Overview

A two-day event 'Trouble in the Woods' took place in April 2024 in Sheffield, and summaries of presentations are available to download from www.ukeconet.org. There are also discussions on the same research website and videoclips of sites on the linked YouTube channel, and my own Blog: https://ianswalkonthewildside.wordpress.com/ . The conference began by celebrating the remarkable and unique heritage of ancient woodlands. To do this we introduced recent and current research in woodland archaeology and management and updates on progress since the landmark publication of the '*Woodland Heritage Manual*' in 2008. Day 2 focussed on the threats to this irreplaceable heritage and ecology posed by current forestry policies and woodland management prescriptions.

Modern machine-driven management of ancient woodlands is causing widespread damage, erosion, degradation, and destruction of a unique heritage resource. This is on a scale not witnessed since the so-called '**Locust Years**' (Oliver Rackham) of forestry in the 1960s and 1970s and which peaked with recognition of forestry-led damage to woodlands, peat bogs, and other habitats in the 1980s and 1990s. The latter caused massive public outcry whereas the present demise of what remain of our ancient woods is passing with barely a murmur. This event asked why this major degradation of our most valuable and valued landscapes is allowed and how come nobody seems remotely aware or concerned. In many cases, centuries of unique heritage, (sometimes thousands of years), and associated ecology are being destroyed in just a few days or even hours. These are the remarkable eco-cultural landscapes so treasured and cherished by the late Oliver Rackham, and about which he did so much to raise public and professional awareness. Yet, almost overnight, much of his legacy is being actively erased from the countryside, and not even the organisations that foster his memory take any action to halt the process.

There is almost no guidance available on the identification and recognition of the woodland resources, and even when they are noted, there is very limited awareness of the extreme vulnerability of the heritage. There is no effective guidance on how to work on site to safeguard the resource and to conserve the woods. What guidance is accessible is full of weasel words where there is talk of 'sustainable' management and 'sustainable coppice working' – but with huge mechanical excavators. Rackham himself argued that mechanised operations in ancient woodlands should be excluded from areas of archaeological interest, but his recommendations go unheeded. In many cases this would of course include the entire land surface of an ancient wood.

Even recognizing and identifying what are ancient woods proves difficult, and in the devolved administrations of the British Isles, the definitions vary in date-line from country to country. More recent reappraisals of ancient woodland inventories in England have provided an opportunity to provide improved guidance, but even this is not widely disseminated.

The aims of this short volume are therefore to try and present succinctly the issues, arguments, and in some cases, possible solutions. Indeed, the discussions at the 2024 event brought together agency workers, conservation bodies, landowners, foresters, local authorities, and woodland enthusiasts, and some excellent ideas and suggestions were made. It is fair to say that overall, there was consensus that there are indeed serious problems, and whilst these are not easy to resolve, there was a willingness to address them.

Nevertheless, with the passing of time and other social and economic issues facing society in general, and a political antipathy and myopia on environmental and heritage issues generally, there has been no active progress on the ground. This volume is an attempt to capture the issues and discussions and to present them to a wider audience. This said, I doubt very much whether the publication will lead to the necessary changes in practice and process, or indeed, any increased awareness in the wider media or by politicians and other decision-makers. I return to some of these issues and my conclusions right at the end of the book. However, it is worth stating at the outset that I see no major, positive outcomes emerging in the near future, and the woodland heritage I am discussing is absolutely irreplaceable and non-tradeable – it is either conserved and safeguarded, or lost forever. New Forestry Commission guidance (October 2024) is certainly helpful but for some reason is only available online (see link at the end of the references) and not as a download, and this will surely reduce its effectiveness. The new Natural England guidance on selection of ancient woodland sites is also a step forwards in baseline information but again may have limited accessibility. That the Forestry Commission has increased its number of Historic Environment Advisors is certainly helpful but much more is needed, and this resource must support both the Commission's own estate and that of private and other public landowners too. In recent years the Woodland Trust has produced an excellent series of booklets on the restoration of ancient woodlands (listed in the references), but in five volumes there is less than one page on woodland archaeology or heritage, and almost zero guidance for a woodland owner or manager on either identification or conservation. Forest Research have also published useful online guidance in terms of the historic environment resources – on woodland and archaeology, and I recognise some of our own work in parts of the materials presented. However, again, the guidance being online only restricts its usefulness and clearly site-based, action research, indicates that it is not yet widely applied.

Serious discussions began with Forestry Commission colleagues and with relevant woodland management and conservation organisations, other agencies, and local authority officers as far back as 2008. However, at the sites where these issues were raised and discussed, significant damage has been ongoing almost annually ever since then and continues today.

Recently discovered World War Two bomb crater in 'The Wood', Graves Park, Sheffield

Context & setting the scene

As archaeologist and woodland champion, John Morris stated when writing of London's woodland archaeology, some years ago (undated), '*Woodlands have been the black hole of archaeology as they have been overlooked by many archaeologists, who often identify likely sites by aerial photography, which the trees hide. Features in woods still exist, as both major and minor earthworks, rather than as buried features in a developed landscape. It is not clear how much woodland archaeology there is, as so little has been surveyed. There is more to be discovered!*'

It is clear that greenspace and particularly woodlands are highly valued by people, and moreover they deliver huge benefits in terms of mental and physical health and wellbeing. I return to people's perceptions of woodlands and why they don't see the damage being done in the final chapter. Much of this benefit and value is associated with 'ancient woodlands' though as far as I am aware, these have not been specifically investigated in depth. A recent Forestry Commission (Forest Research) report (Saraev *et al.*, 2021), provides details of values associated with access to woodlands.

The report summarises the benefits as follows: '*Access to woodlands is very important for individuals to support their mental health and well-being. However, these benefits have yet to be included in natural capital accounts at national level. This study is the first attempt to provide national estimates of the natural capital value of the mental health benefits provided by UK woodlands. .... It is based upon an association between regular visits to natural environments and a reduced prevalence of common mental illnesses, combined with societal costs of depression and anxiety, including lost working days and NHS costs.'*

The introduction provides some key data.

'The annual mental health benefits associated with visits to the UK's woodlands are estimated to be £185 million (at 2020 prices). Country-level values based on population size (rounded to the nearest million) are £141 million for England, £26 million for Scotland, £13 million for Wales and £6 million for Northern Ireland. The values are based on evidence of the reduced incidence of depression and anxiety as a result of regular visits to nature. We draw upon evidence regarding the number of regular visitors to woodlands, and the prevalence of mental health conditions in the general population, to estimate the numbers of cases of depression and anxiety that may be reduced. The avoided costs are based upon the average annual costs to society of living with depression or anxiety. These comprise costs associated with treatment, including visits to GPs, drug prescriptions, inpatient care and social services. They also include employment-related costs based on estimates of the number of working days lost due to mental health issues.'

This confirms and quantifies much of what is already known about proximity to, and access to woodland and the life enhancement that brings. We know that even seeing woods and trees makes us happier and healthier and for patients in hospital in a post-op recovery situation for example, or in other stressful circumstances, they get better faster and more effectively. American environmental psychologist, Roger Ulrich, in the early 1990s put forward the 'Stress Reduction Theory' (or SRT) which suggested that humans have two basic reactions to views of the natural world: 1) A preference for natural scenes, 2) When nature is viewed, we develop a 'positively toned emotional state', i.e., we feel better. Moreover, his team's studies indicated that these triggered actual physiological responses that meant quicker recovery, and such effects were absent from strictly urban experiences. Of course, in countries such as Japan the therapeutic benefits of 'forest bathing' have long been recognised. Since the earlier studies further work has strengthened this position, and more recent research even demonstrated major impacts on childhood development of memory and cognition. In Great Britain, Dr Wiliam Bird has pioneered approaches to health based around these ideas, and the impacts of our trees and woods on health, wellbeing, and the economy are now indisputable.

Wood anemone in ancient woodland

Living close to mature woodland even adds value to property and increases the 'desire to reside' in a particular location. These observations confirm that the value of effectively managed and conserved ancient woodlands is huge, and that this is not just 'virtual' value but real costs for bodies such as the National Health Service, to name just one. With all this in mind (and there is plenty of good research to back up these assertions) then it seems strange, at least to me, that we manage the woods so badly and often in ignorance of what they really are. In Chapter 2, I write about how 'when you walk through an ancient wood you tread in the footsteps of innumerable ghosts of people that lived and worked there over centuries', and it is this somehow indefinable patina of history and time that makes a woodland 'ancient'. Bearing this in mind, I advocate that we should walk gently through the woods and forests with a nod to the ghosts and shadows of the past, rather than stomping through in hobnailed boots. The rich ecologies and biodiversity of ancient woods and the consequences of their histories and heritage is what delivers and provides the health and wellbeing that so many crave. So, for our benefits and those of future generations, and the diversity of countless other species too, we should care better for the woods. We are merely the short-term custodians and what we wantonly destroy is lost for those who follow, and they will not even be aware of what has been taken from them. I know people who are active members of woodland conservation bodies but now shun their local woods because of the devastation of recent management. Surely, this cannot be right.

As I note in Chapter 4, almost all the woodland and tree professionals I have met over the last forty years or so, are passionate about what they do, and indeed often simply don't see the damage. Maybe they choose not to see it, and in a tiny minority of cases they are simply doing a job for money, and really don't care, but this is rare indeed. So, what I and other landscape historians or landscape ecologists, and more experienced archaeologists view as catastrophic, irretrievable damage, many forestry practitioners, feel is acceptable. Conservation managers are often simply unaware that they are managing an historic landscape with important eco-cultural heritage. Two barriers to recognition are seeing the countryside in one case (of ecologists and conservation managers), as simply a mix of agglomerations of species forming communities without understanding environmental and land-use history that underpins it. In the other case (of archaeologists), the countryside is viewed and recorded as a series of individual monuments rather than a coherent whole. Whereas in practice the upstanding, visible 'monuments' are indicative of layers of historic features sometimes laid down one over another spanning many centuries. The idea that you can simply avoid the obvious features and thus avoid significant damage is nonsense. A final point of context, is that with woodlands there is little need to rush to management decisions or actions, since these are long-term, continuous ventures. Current management always seems to be in a hurry; that in the past was carried out over generations.

Charcoal burner's hut, Markash, New Forest, 1920s

Preamble

It seems useful, logical, and sensible to begin an account of woodland conservation management and contemporary issues with some key definitions from the *Shorter Oxford English Dictionary*.

Conservation: This is a fundamental concept in terms of the last fifty years or so of environmental management, but sometimes it feels we have lost sight of its meaning. It is 'the action of conserving; preservation from destructive influences, decay or waste', or in other words, caring.

Heritage: 'Heritage' is a property, something that is inherited, passed down from previous generations. In the case of 'cultural heritage,' this doesn't mean money or property, but culture, values, and traditions and include both 'tangible' (i.e., physical objects, artefacts, or monuments), and 'intangible' (i.e., memories, traditions, and practices).

Wood / woodland: The dictionary definition is, 'a collection of trees growing more or less thickly together, especially naturally as distinct from a plantation'. It is 'usually larger than a grove or copse, but includes these, and smaller than a forest'. Woodland is ground covered with trees.

Ancient woodland: In Britain 'ancient woodland' is that which can be evidenced to have originated before specific date (which differs from country to country) but is generally from around 1600AD to the late 1700s. There is a broad assumption that if a wood was present at this time, then its origins pre-date widespread tree-planting, and therefore the woodland has been present for several centuries at least and is semi-natural or natural in character. When sites are identified and confirmed, then they may be added to the 'Ancient Woodland Inventory' which has become a mechanism for a degree of statutory protection from development. This protection has no bearing on site management and consequent damage which may undermine the wood's 'ancient' character, and long-term, its status.

Forest: This means 'an extensive tract of land covered with trees and undergrowth sometimes intermingled with pasture'. But 'royal forests' were areas of land set aside for hunting by the king, populated with wild game and 'protected' as such. These lands were subject to the 'Forest Laws' and in some cases might have few trees.

Forestry: A dictionary definition is, 'the science and art of forming and cultivating forests and the management of growing timber'. This applies to the modern concept of forestry which emerged largely in France, Austria, and Germany, in the 1700s and 1800s, and differs from the royal forest and from 'woodmanship'. The latter means the looking after trees in a wood or forest, the felling or lopping of trees for timber or fuel, and the selling or purveying of wood. Woodmanship was the craft industry that emerged during the medieval period with largely oral traditions passed down through generations and was the management of enclosed, medieval woods until the 1800s and 1900s. Forestry grew as a practice in Britain during the late 1700s, throughout the 1800s, and especially in the twentieth century following the post-World War One establishment of the Forestry Commission.

Sustainability: This is the idea that goods and services should be produced in ways that do not use resources which cannot be replaced and do not damage the environment. The term which has ground in usage since the 1987 'Brundtland Report' and the 1992 Rio Convention, implies the avoidance of depletion of natural resources so as to maintain ecological balance, and relates to the aspiration of 'the pursuit of global environmental sustainability'.

The Locust Years: These are years of hardship or poverty, such as the biblical locust years when the harvests of the people of Zion were wiped out for four years, eaten by the locusts. Famously, Winston Churchill called the 1930s 'the locust years' as a reference to the appalling losses, mistakes, and failures which devoured any hope of peace during the tragic decade leading to World War Two.

Wild garlic in ancient woodland, Moss Valley, Derbyshire

Acknowledgements

I am very grateful to Professor Paul Adam for reminding me that Oliver Rackham described the post-Second World War period of British forestry as 'The Locust Years' and thus inspiring the title of this volume. Professor Joan Maloof kindly agreed to my quoting extensively from her book' '*Nature's Temples*'. Colleagues and friends too numerous to mention have, over many years, worked with me on woodland and tree issues, and both Christine Handley and Dr Paul Ardron have been particularly supportive. The late Professors Melvyn Jones and Donald Pigott provided direction to my earlier work in the field, and of course, the late, great Professor Oliver Rackham was an inspiration. My wife Liz has tolerated my obsession.

Charcoal burners at Coniston, English Lake District, 1920s

Ancient oak-tree, Moss Valley, Derbyshire

Chapter 1: Introduction: The nature of treescapes

Ancient woods are not pristine 'natural' places but eco-cultural landscapes, 'worked' for countless centuries by men and women with oxen and horsepower alone. The communities of woodmen and women left their mark, but this was as palimpsests of humanity ingrained into the long-term patina of the ancient countryside. When we walk through an ancient woodland today, we do so in the footsteps, and shadows of the ghosts of these people. This contrasts with the modern 'worked' woods which involve few people passing through as itinerant machine-drivers before moving on to their next assignment. Great tracked vehicles rip through earthwork heritage, ecology, soils, and anciently worked trees. Both types of woods, (ancient and modern), are 'worked' but only the first ('traditionally worked woods') are now 'ancient woods'. Modern management 'works' the woods but industrially and they lose both antiquity and continuity (the unfathomable essence of ancient woods). These sites are no longer 'ancient woods' but 'industrial woods', different, distinctive, and degraded. Once the antiquity of soils, heritage, worked trees, and vegetation are compromised, then clearly the woodland is no longer an 'ancient wood'. Oliver Rackham compared this to the ancient medieval wood being like an antique illuminated manuscript on parchment with the notes, scribbles and additions overlaid through countless centuries, as a palimpsest. Modern management erodes and erases this to smudge and merge the manuscript and spewing out at the end, a cheap modern paperback novel. Imagine this is effect as turning a medieval illuminated script into a Jeffrey Archer novel ...... Such degraded landscapes cannot be considered genuinely ancient woodland .... This we must recognise and is the consequence of the aforementioned management.

Birkett-Foster the Wood-wain

Key issues and themes included the following:

- The unique nature, heritage, & archaeology of ancient woodlands.

- New and emerging research on woodland heritage and archaeology

- The differences between archaeology '*of*' the woods, and archaeology '*in*' the woods.

- The limited recognition of archaeology and heritage in woods.

- Links between ancient woodland ecology and heritage.

- The vulnerability of woodland heritage features.

- The absence of any due process of guidance for physical management operations in woodland environments.

- The damage done to heritage by modern machine-driven site management of woodlands.

- Shortcomings in the Ancient Woodland Inventory (AWI).

- A recognition of traditionally worked woods and the separation of industrial woods – and their necessary removal from the Inventory, perhaps replaced by a category of 'Industrial Woodlands'.

Outcomes from the 2024 meeting: Our aspiration was to reach a shared vision of common ground and to agree ways forward which protect and conserve these unique, ancient landscapes in the future. Moreover, a further hope was to reawaken wider community awareness of ancient woods, their ecology, history archaeology, and heritage, much as did the late, great scholars, Oliver Rackham and Melvyn Jones. In this regard, the event was dedicated to four great servants and pioneers of research in landscape and ecological history with strong Sheffield connections: Professor Melvyn Jones, Dr Frank Spode, Professor Donald Pigott, and Professor David Hey. They are all sadly missed, and in the event, we remembered and celebrated their achievements.

Bluebell - Typical ancient woodland indicator plant, Moss Valley, Derbyshire

Chapter 2: What is a 'wood'?

Trees, woodlands, and woods are very much in the news as solutions to everything from slowing the flow of floodwaters, to mitigating climate change impacts through carbon capture, and increasing environmental resilience to environmental changes. However, when discussions about treescapes take place, or they are considered in policies or in the media, there is little attention paid to detail in terms of the different types of tree-dominated landscapes. Yet the implications of the specific treescape can be radically different in terms of their environmental impacts but also with regard to the potential intrinsic vulnerability. The latter relates to their heritage and archaeology, and associated with or even dependent on these, their soils and biodiversity. Therefore, with so much in the media about planting woods and trees, it is worth asking some key questions and maybe sorting out definitions. Only then can we really assess and evaluate some of the major and pressing environmental issues of our times.

Foxgloves in ancient woodland

A preamble to this, is that across England at least, observations suggest very strongly that despite the widely-read works of that pioneer of ancient woodland, the late Professor Oliver Rackham, few woods are managed to conserve their heritage. This is both remarkable and sad, since the work of historians such as Oliver and Sheffield's own the late Professor Melvyn Jones demonstrated the unique cultural heritage of former medieval woods. Moreover, studies by scholars like George Peterken, Keith Kirby, Tom Williamson, and even myself, demonstrate connections between history and site ecology or biodiversity. Mixing human history and nature, these landscapes are what I describe as 'eco-cultural' with human impact acting on sites and soils over many centuries to influence trees and other biodiversity. Indeed, this is what make an ancient woods different and distinctive from all other treescapes. These sites have continuity and connectivity over many centuries whilst at the same time being dynamic living entities. A consequence of this unique lineage is that they are specific to a place and are absolutely irreplaceable. There is a further complication however, that once part of the human cultural landscape, the working countryside, these treescapes have experienced 'cultural severance' with ending of traditional and subsistence usage. This change from 'working woods' to 'amenity woods', or else 'leisurely landscapes', has implications for their sustainability and for how we perceive them. Most woods today are viewed by people as 'natural' or 'wild', which they are not.

Since the pioneering work of Rackham and Peterken in the 1970s and 1980s, followed by a body of other scholars locally, nationally, and internationally, there was an awakening of consciousness about the special values of 'ancient woods'. Through this work and associated discussions, there was a growing understanding of the specific issues, histories, and ecologies of ancient woods framed in more intimate detail. Indeed, because of this, it is now possible to place the ancient woods more roundly in their ecological and historical context. Nevertheless, there is now a further complication is the apparently rapid loss of cultural and professional knowledge as a generation of researchers and professionals has retired or otherwise been lost. Newly-emerging professionals as site managers for conservation bodies have often missed out on the discussions described above, have limited relevant training from college or university, and increasingly rely on contemporary social media sources for information and awareness-raising. This loss of corporate and professional memory is not a totally new phenomenon and indeed has been documented previously with woods in Sheffield for example. In this case, woods traditionally managed for charcoal burning from medieval times up to the 1900s, by the 1960s, were believed to be two-hundred-year-old plantations. However, the implications of the current changes are that site managers frequently have limited experience of woodland management and often no awareness of history, heritage, and sensitivity. This is a recipe for very damaging operations in some of our most precious conservation sites.

Ancient wood in Derbyshire's Moss Valley

Treescapes: woods, woodlands, plantations, & forests

To understand an ancient wood, we firstly need to examine the term 'wood', and this is in the context of treescapes or woodlands that include diverse sites and types of ecological systems. In establishing conservation and management priorities, it is important to understand the types of natural, semi-natural, or eco-cultural woodlands and how they differ from merely planted trees. Basically, plantations are as they imply sites where trees have been deliberately planted and in Britain and Europe, this practice was not commonplace before around 1600 to 1700 AD. It creates 'plantations' and these may be onto a previously non-woodland site or into and perhaps replacing existing woodland. (In

27

England the latter are sometimes called PAWS or 'Planted Ancient Woodland Sites'). Originating in continental Europe in the eighteenth century, 'forestry' is the science and practice of establishing and managing such plantations and is totally separate from the term 'forest'. Confusingly, this word may mean either a naturally-occurring (but often managed) treescape or else is an area of land over which medieval forest laws applied. In the latter cases, these were largely hunting lands and might (though not always) be relatively open land and free of trees or at least with only limited closed-canopy woodland. The medieval forests were wood-pastures related to medieval deer parks, medieval chases, and often neglected, wooded commons, as places that mixed production of timber, wood, and use by grazing animals. The modern scientific 'forestry' is very different from the cultural traditions of 'woodmanship' as practiced by rural craftworkers for centuries.

OLD OAKS ON WICKHAM COMMON KENT.

Old oaks on Wickham Common, Kent, early 1900s

Different from a plantation is a 'wood' which in England at least, is generally an area of treescape enclosed (or protected) by a bank and ditch with a wall, hedge, paling, fence, or dead-hedge, and then named within the manorial estate. Such woods had trees encircled by a boundary to exclude grazing livestock and within this enclosure there was management for timber (cut maybe every 80 to 120 years), and underwood or coppice (cut every 10 to 25 years). These sites were mostly established during the period of two to three centuries after the Norman Conquest (1066) the changes are apparent in reading the Domesday account (1086) and considering the countryside before and after that time. Prior to Domesday most of the woodland in the English countryside was open wood-pasture with little enclosed coppice wood. Undoubtedly during the Saxon and Viking times trees were coppiced and wood was harvested, but

29

this was not in the organised and intensive way that was developed after the Norman Conquest. It is also believed that some early 'woods' were only temporarily protected by short-term dead-hedges to allow young coppice to 'spring' or 'sprout' from the cut stools. Probably over time, and as systems of management became more sophisticated, sites were protected by more permanent barriers. Such 'woods' were either coppice-with-standards (underwood and timber trees) or simple coppice (i.e., lacking the standard timber trees). Whilst most resulting 'ancient woods' were Norman or post-Norman in origin, some were established in the Saxon countryside. Coppicing undoubtedly occurred in the earlier landscape, even in prehistoric times (perhaps with people copying the natural coppicing of native beavers and of some trees like lime, alder, and willow), but was in extensive treescapes and not in designated protected sites. The Romans certainly coppiced woods more formally but whether this extended into and through the post-Roman period is uncertain. Indeed, the balance between managed coppice woods and multi-functional wood-pastures often reflects the extent of the landscape resource and the size of the human population dependent on it. Before Domesday, the English population was relatively sparce in an extensive, wood-pasture-dominated countryside which was relatively resource-rich. After Domesday, the population rose rapidly during the subsequent centuries and the woodland resource, essential for survival in a pre-petrochemical world, became increasingly scarce. Protection by enclosure with regular coppice and timber cycles helped ensure sustainable supplies of vital materials at the parish or manorial level. From Domesday onwards, if the wood survived and was used, then this management often continued over many centuries and sometimes into the nineteenth or twentieth century. At this time, many traditional woods were lost to urban development or farming, converted to high forest plantations, or simply abandoned.

In terms of heritage and archaeological interest, this longevity of history is important. Within a formally coppiced wood there will be evidence of human activities and even settlement in terms of internal and external ditches and banks and associated walls. The working coppice wood will have hut bases from woodland workers, and earthworks associated with cutting, processing, and storing of timber and underwood, and often multi-stemmed remnants from former coppice trees. (Some woodland oaks in the latter category may be 800 to 1,000 years old, and in the case of lime trees, much older). There may also be remains from pre-woodland activities including Romano-British walls and earthworks, Romano-British villas, trackways and other features, such as prehistoric fields, buildings and enclosures, marked stones, and much more. A key point in all of this is that the remains and the evidence of past occupation and usage are made up of earth, stones, and rocks, with soils and sediments, and associated ecology. As such, the heritage is exceedingly vulnerable and indeed, it has largely been removed from the countryside beyond the wood. Essentially, what remains in the woods (and perhaps on fragments of heaths, moors, and commons), is almost our entire resource of heritage overlain down the centuries as palimpsests in the landscape. Where these working enclosed 'woods' survive today they are the 'ancient woods'.

Working the woods, early 1900s

As explained above, these 'woods' were mostly but not always, enclosed from some sort of wood-pasture or else from common open fields of the medieval landscape. If they survived the vagaries of history, especially the early industrial period's parliamentary enclosures, and then twentieth-century intensification of agriculture and impacts of private and corporate forestry, then these are our 'ancient woods' today. Their origins are reflected in contemporary ecology and biodiversity, and when you walk through an ancient wood you tread in the footsteps of innumerable ghosts of people that lived and worked there over centuries. Not purely 'natural' but these are 'eco-cultural' landscapes reflecting people, nature, and time.

Medieval charcoal hearth in the Derbyshire's Moss Valley Long Wood damaged by management

Because they were enclosed and managed as described, many ancient woods preserved elements of much earlier countryside including evidence of woodland workers and their families over nearly 1,000 years. There may be 'earth-fast' stones, carved Bronze Age boulders (cup-and-ring marked stones), formerly 'worked' now retired 'working trees' such as pollards (high coppice), stubs (on ancient boundaries), and coppices. The sites range from traditionally-managed rural woods to intensively-managed early industrial woods the latter often around industrial centres and producing charcoal for metal working and other uses, and sometimes 'white coal' specifically for lead smelting. The impacts of these sometimes intensive activities vary from site to site and with the longevity and intensity of usage. In woods used to make charcoal and whitecoal, there may be tens or even hundreds of charcoal hearths and so-called Q-pits. These will be close to trackways, building sites, hearths, and processing or storage areas. In some cases, the modern vegetation is totally a reflection of this history of usage, and in some woods intensively used for charcoal manufacture, almost all topsoil was removed. These are examples of the unique, site-specific, timelines of nature and people which have created the so-called palimpsests or multi-layered landscapes of history.

Cup-and-ring marked stone from Bronze age or Neolithic, Ecclesall Woods, Sheffield

In neighbourhood woods for instance, you can often walk back through landscapes of history perhaps extending over 3,000 years or more. Across the wider countryside, this has long-since been erased by humanity's modern living, making our surviving woods uniquely important cultural heritage and irreplaceable markers of our biodiversity and history. At regional and local levels, the ancient woods frequently have distinctive ecologies and patterns of usage reflecting patterns of human use for local industries and biogeographical influences. This is living history on the doorstep of many communities.

Often unseen: the remarkable history & heritage of ancient woods, trees, & forests

The remarkable timelines of woodland environmental history and the associated cultural heritage (tangible and intangible) were first noted by researchers such as Oliver Rackham and George Peterken in the 1970s. They also coined the term 'ancient woodlands' as distinct from 'wildwood' or 'primary woodland' which they also considered. These were anciently working woods, and following from Rackham's pioneering work in particular, researchers around Britain and across Europe delved into the history, heritage, and ecology of 'ancient woods'. Leading scholars have included Chris Smout at St Andrews, Tom Williamson at the University of East Anglia, Della Hooke at Birmingham, Richard Muir at York St John, and Charles Watkins at Nottingham, together with others and many across Europe.

The process was a steep learning curve and for example, on the field trip to Ecclesall Woods associated with the 1992 woodland conference *'Ancient Woodlands: Their Archaeology and Ecology – a coincidence of interest'*, in Sheffield, it is fair to say that the assembled 'experts' including eminent archaeologists mistook much of what they saw on site. Thirty years on and we have a much fuller appreciation of the site and its heritage, although more is discovered every year. Nevertheless, the event demonstrated the paucity of information, understanding, and interdisciplinary collaboration at that time. However, the conference served as a stepping stone to a major European meeting in 2003 *'Working and Walking in the Footsteps of Ghosts'*, also held in Sheffield. This was followed by further seminars and programmes of workshops to produce the *'Woodland Heritage Manual'*, and then to develop additional guidance and to expand the conceptual frameworks.

Remains of revetted charcoal platform, probably 1700s, Cumbria

In the Sheffield area, as described by Rackham, a 'school' of woodland historians and ecologists emerged around the work of Melvyn Jones, but also of historian David Hey, ecologist Oliver Gilbert, and the earlier woodland botanists such as Donald Pigott, and Philip Grime. Sheffield became a centre for such collaborative landscape-based studies through the Landscape Conservation Forum with national and international meetings held in 1992, and then in 2003. Subsequent workshops led to the publication of the landmark *'Woodland Heritage Manual'* in 2008. Along with the emergence of the Ancient Tree Forum, key concepts were developed over this period.

Coppice with wild garlic, Suffolk

Critical conceptual issues have emerged and developed including:

1) Ancient woodland concepts.

2) Working woods as opposed to 'wildwood'.

3) Working trees and retired veterans.

4) Ancient woodland indicator species.

5) The archaeology *in* woods, and the archaeology *of* woods.

6) The eco-cultural nature of woods.

7) The importance of the 1235 Act of Commons – *'The Magna Carta of the landscape'*.

8) Tangible and intangible cultural heritage of woodlands.

9) Ideas of Shadow Woods, Ghost Woods, and lost landscapes.

10) Issues of continuity and antiquity in land-use timelines.

11) The occurrence even in urban ancient woods, of features dating back to medieval or even prehistory.

12) The importance of veteran and ancient trees.

13) The largely unrecognised ages of ancient coppices and clones.

Other matters arising (see the *Woodland Heritage Manual* for instance), included:

1) A general lack of awareness of woodland heritage by archaeologists and historians.

2) A generally limited awareness of woodland heritage, archaeology, and history by ecologists.

3) Broadly a lack of communication between key disciplines inducing practical foresters.

4) The need for cross-disciplinary and multi-disciplinary research and guidance to understand anciently wooded landscapes more fully.

5) Limited teaching of relevant topics at universities or colleges.

6) The need for accessible and robust guidance for surveyors, site managers and forestry operatives.

7) A need for best practice guidance / training for minimal impact forestry operations on-site.

8) Limited awareness by practitioners of the delicate nature and vulnerability of woodland heritage.

9) The emergence of improved guidance and practice on managing veteran pollards and maiden trees, but little in the way of information on coppices and clones.

There also emerged differences in views as to whether or not ancient woods should be actively managed and potential conflicts in conservation interest between botanical aspects and say, deadwood invertebrates. This was reflected in the emerging understanding of the divergence between historically enclosed 'woods' and 'wood-pastures'. In recent years, the relationships between treescapes and rewilding projects have triggered debates about grazing impacts, and between natural regeneration and artificial planting of trees.

Charcoal burner's monument in Ecclesall Woods, Sheffield, 1786

A major observation to emerge through decades of research is that medieval 'woods', along perhaps with some heaths and commons, provide and protect unique archives of both human occupation and of associated ecology. These are eco-culturally rich places when much of the historically-derived heritage and ecology has been destroyed in the surrounding landscape. This unique resource is made up of the humps and bumps in woodland soils and sediments, in earth-fast stones, in portable antiquities, in the flora and fauna of the woodland, and in the living (especially historically-managed or 'working') trees. In many places, these represent the last, irreplaceable, and precious remnants of the ancient countryside celebrated by the late Oliver Rackham.

The 2024 conference presentations explored some of these issues and the emerging discoveries though the application of new technologies such as LiDAR and computer mapping.

Complex of prehistoric barrows discovered in Square Plantation near Ecclesall Woods, Sheffield, 2023

Ancient, paved trackway through Ecclesall Woods, Sheffield

Chapter 3: Trouble in the woods

Forestry vehicle tracks cut deeply through the ancient monument in Whitwell Wood, 2009, and judged as acceptable by the Forestry Commission

Understanding the issues and problems for the effective conservation of ancient woods, begins with the official 'Ancient Woodland Inventories' and even with 'Ancient Tree Inventories'. This is in part because these were never designed to assume the planning and guiding functions that they now have, and whilst they are currently under review, many wooded sites have been wrongly attributed or overlooked. Indeed, physical 'cultural' heritage is frequently ignored or unrecognised for what it is, and the living 'biocultural heritage' of say a 500-year old coppiced oak or a 1,000-year old clonal

43

holly for example, is often cleared away with barely a second thought. Furthermore, re-planting after woodland clearance does not help this, does not replace it, and may turn a 'wood' into a 'plantation'. With a lot of luck and maybe 500 years of history, such a site might become something resembling an ancient 'wood', but perhaps not.

A key point from the earlier chapter, '*What is a Wood?*', is that whilst past woodland management might have been quite intensive, it occurred in long-term, predictable cycles often over many centuries. Furthermore, the process of coppicing and felling, with a boom-bust of light and dark, selected out the species of plants and animals which we now know as 'ancient woodland indicators'. Additionally, such work continuous over centuries, was undertaken by sheer brute force of (mostly) men, and their animals – horses, ponies, and oxen. These processes continued to an extent into the earlier days of modern forestry in the 1800s and early 1900s. However, there were major changes in process and scale of operations from the establishment of the British Forestry Commission following World War One timber shortages, with the demise of many remaining rural crafts, depopulation of the English countryside in the 1920s and 1930s, and then the importation of American heavy machinery such as tracked vehicles in the Second World War and the period that followed. These were game-changers in terms of woodland management and its impacts, and their effects can be traced back from the pre-petrochemically subsidised age of woodmanship of the early 1800s, through to the 1950s.

Vehicle tracks through the ancient and heritage-rich Whitwell Wood, winter 2020

A consequence of the post-World War Two period of 'improvement' and the appliance of new technologies was massive destruction. This led Oliver Rackham to describe the period of forestry from the 1950s to the 1980s as the 'Locust Years' for woodlands in the UK. Great numbers of medieval woods that had survived until that time were swept away. However, with the post-War rise of conservation and environmentalism, it seemed these adverse impacts on woodland heritage declined. This was in part with changing forestry guidance from the intensive afforestation of the 1970s and 1980s, reaction to public outcry over damage and forestry-related tax-breaks, and growing recognition of what became known as 'ancient woods'. The latter was a term developed and refined by Oliver Rackham and George Peterken, and which became enshrined in British conservation policy triggering the emergence of conservation NGOs such as the Woodland Trust. My own discussions with foresters from the 1960s, confirmed that they ploughed-out features such as prehistoric hilltop enclosures from the countryside as they drained and planted exotic conifers. Furthermore, whilst the individuals realised the damage that was being done, but it was simply what they were told to do, and they did it. Nevertheless, whilst the damage wrought on countryside heritage was severe, it was to an extent limited by the mode of practice on the ground which still relied on numbers of men working with chainsaws and small tractors clearing sites of pre-existing woodland. As Rackham later noted, the ecological components of some of these replanted woodland sites proved quite resilient in their recovery. The heritage on the other hand was often terminally compromised, and Rackham made strong recommendations that sensitive archaeology should be identified and then avoided during machine-based site operations. This clearly is not the case today.

By the 1990s, there was a step away from publicly-funded forestry on heaths, peat-bogs, and ancient woodland sites, and it seemed that conservation had turned a corner. Yet within just a few decades, there has been a corporate and cultural loss of memory and awareness of the unique values, history, and ecology of ancient woods, and a drive to manage 'neglected' sites. This seems to be driven by a general desire to interfere rather than to conserve, and particularly to remove 'diseased' trees (always a bug-bear of the Forestry Commission), and to plant new trees rather than to manage natural processes of regeneration. These are complicated matters, and I have written about them in detail elsewhere. However, there is a sobering observation which scales-up the type of damage now being wreaked, for whatever reason. In these 'New Locust Years' for our ancient woods, the operations on site are undertaken by individual workers in huge, often tracked, vehicles. In order to remove cut timber, access roads like motorways are cut through and surfaced to facilitate big lorries operating. This includes large turning circles and parking areas within medieval woodland boundaries and even undertaken by woodland conservation NGOs. In many cases, the timber extraction makes no profit and often is mandated by Defra because a notifiable disease has been reported within a certain distance of the site. Very often it is the vehicle ingress to the site, the construction of roadways, and the physical taking of timber out that cause the damage, and yet frequently these are done only in order to pay the costs of extraction. Indeed, if diseased trees were found on site and simply ring-barked or felled by chainsaw and left on site, the damage would be negligible, and the costs would be a fraction of those now incurred. The carbon capture and deadwood biodiversity would also be enhanced. This current practice is madness, and a final irony is that in most instances the action to contain or to eliminate the spread of tree diseases, fails to do so. Yet there is an imperative 'to do something' even if it is costly, damaging, and doesn't work, but is justified by vague ideas of 'sustainability'. The waves of pests and diseases are clearly triggered by processes of climate change, environmental stresses including atmospheric nitrogen deposition, and globalisation. Drastic site disturbance and stress in our woodlands simply makes things worse. Furthermore, it seems that there is not time or expertise for effective prior survey of site heritage, and existing management plans and agreements are 'trumped' by massive disease control operations.

Timber extraction, Whitwell Wood, Derbyshire

Today's foresters often justify their intensive operations because 'these have always been working woods'. Indeed, this reawakening of the historic nature of the working woods emerged from the studies of historians like Oliver Rackham and Melvyn Jones. However, this is a misunderstanding of the history, and the foresters fail to compare like with like. Rather than continuing the traditions as old woodmen used to do, the modern way with few workers and huge machines, simple erases what went before – i.e., the unique traces and evidence of nature and people over thousands of years. As explained previously, this heritage is unique and irreplaceable. The old ways left their scars in the woods which we now regard as heritage, but they also preserved unique patinas and traceries of ecology and a way of life extending back through time. Modern forestry work wipes the slate clean, levels out the palimpsest, and creates a new, industrial, bland treescape often justified as 'conservation'; it is nothing of the sort. In a sort of Orwellian 'double-speak' we use 'low impact' vehicles and machines which in practice grind down earthworks and flatten standing stones to erase all that has gone before. Multi-stemmed former coppices sometimes many centuries old, are cleared in just a few minutes often in the name of forest hygiene or conservation best practice.

Exposed charcoal from hearth, Whitwell Wood, Derbyshire, 2009

Why does this destruction happen even when the heritage is known?

Essentially, even with raised awareness of the importance of ancient woods, whilst sometimes the heritage is known, for specific sites this resource is often not surveyed. Oliver Rackham and Melvyn Jones particularly, triggered a revolution in awareness and thinking about ancient woods and their heritage. Then, with help from the Heritage Lottery, the Forestry Commission, English Heritage, and the Woodland Trust, back in 2008 we produced the *Woodland Heritage Manual*.

Forestry access routes cut through the woodland and ancient monument, Whitwell, Derbyshire, 2009

Yet the importance of this remarkable heritage and archaeology is still ignored, damaged, destroyed, and eroded with most woodland management driven by established forestry practice sometimes with ecological

51

influences too. Little thought is given to 'heritage' and archaeology. A significant compounding problem is that most formally trained archaeologists do not recognise the archaeology '*of*' woodland management, and little is recorded in the local authority recording systems. This is the system that triggers consultations on proposals for site work. So, although woodland heritage is far more sensitive than ecology (being easily displaced stones and humps and bumps in the soils) and is irreplaceable, modern management rarely considers it. Yet it is this eco-cultural patina that influences and maintains the remarkable ecologies of ancient woods, and it is the character which makes them 'ancient'.

Burnt out veteran tree in the Moss Valley woodlands, North Derbyshire

Rough Standhills, Sheffield PAWS unsurveyed ancient wood and wood-pasture cleared 2023 (above, below, and following)

For conservation bodies, the idea of 'conserving' through custodianship but not actively managing a site, i.e., allowing nature to be free-willed and protecting cultural heritage, seems contrary to current thinking. This is despite free-willed nature being an underpinning principle of much rewilding. Ecological change in woods is inherently a slow process and generally, there is little reason to rush into ill-informed, damaging management operations. Throughout history, managing a woodland has been a long-term process and commitment and so there is no need to rush in. However, the tendency today is: 1) to fail to consult widely with experts, 2) to fail to consult with the public, and to work within an approved and agreed *management plan*, and 3) to fail to develop the latter based on the necessary and appropriate surveys of history, heritage, and ecology. And yet there is no real need to rush into damaging operations. Current practice of issuing 'Statutory Plant Health Notices' (SPHNs) issued by the Forestry Commission under direction from Defra, however, does seem to over-ride all other constraints and protocols (such as surveys and management plans) even when applied apparently beyond the scope of the legal order.

Overall, most modern woodland and forestry site management is driven by traditional silviculture practice but with some aspirations towards nature conservation, and increasingly the delivery of active outdoor recreation and sports. Indeed, some wildlife conservation NGOs when challenged on site damage caused by construction of recreational cycle tracks inside ancient woods, simply stated that they are 'leisure organisations' rather than conservation bodies. If that is so, then who are the advocates for nature and heritage? In this scenario, irreparable damage can easily occur as poorly-known or unrecorded biocultural heritage is erased, eroded, and removed. With major cuts to local authority countryside services over recent decades, there has been widespread change in practice from in-depth, carefully researched and consulted management plans in the past, and now to often gung-ho, short-term implementation of practical works sometimes simply driven by a desire to do something even if wrong (the 'David Cameron badger cull logic'). This exacerbates an already challenging situation for the future of these remarkable heritage palimpsests.

Even when effective surveys have been undertaken, there is often a gulf between the evaluation and the practitioners undertaking work on the ground. If damage is to be avoided, then the guidance of the '*Woodland Heritage Manual*' and more recent notes on working practices on site, need to be applied. Importantly, operatives need to be briefed on the ground, with vulnerable sub-sites marked up, safe extraction routes for timber, and access routes for vehicles identified. In ancient woods, work by machines should be with ultra-low-impact vehicles. Present-day working with heavy machines converts '***traditionally-managed ancient woods***' into '***industrially-managed woods***' or even '***post-industrial woods***' and yet grant-aid and site protection in planning do not reflect these altered states.

Designation and consequent funding should relate to the real site status and condition. Recognition of status and of good practice would help, but at present there are no accepted standards or forestry kite-marks for sustainable cultural heritage, and the timber quality kite marks are not fit for purpose when it comes to heritage. A big problem is that current official guidance from Defra and the Forestry Commission does not take these issues into account and grant-aid steers projects into damaging actions. Most conservation bodies, primarily led by ecological and leisure practice, simply get it wrong, and this situation must be addressed if ancient woods are to be effectively conserved.

Modern vehicular access road through ancient woodland, Moss Valley, North Derbyshire

The impacts of large vehicles in ancient woodlands

I have raised issues of vehicle impacts in a number of papers and articles. This note is intended to summarise succinctly the main reasons for concern, and to explain why such management converts **'traditionally-managed ancient woods'**, into **'industrially-managed woods'**. I fully understand that this may be a process that is now impossible to stop – for commercial forestry reasons. However, the impacts of these damaging operations should then be recognised in site designation and in any publicly-funded grant aid. The latter should clearly be higher for the intact traditionally-managed sites. And of course, the changed status of these woods should be recognised in publicly-accessible inventories such as the **'Ancient Woodland Inventory'**. However, this notice should not reduce statutory protection from development for designated ancient woods but rather give increased protection status and funding to traditionally-managed sites.

Modern vehicular access through Long Wood, Moss Valley, North Derbyshire cutting through medieval charcoal hearths

So, why the concern?

Ancient woods have been **worked** for centuries as coppice of coppice-with-standards, and this is well documented. Furthermore, such management over time did alter the ecology and the landscape in these 'eco-cultural' sites. People and their animals lived in and around the woods and these areas were critically important to the local economy. However, the woods being worked was by people and animal-power until the middle of the twentieth century. The woodmen and women left their mark in the vegetation and the soils, rocks, and other features. Each layer of activity since antiquity was overlaid one over the others in what we described as a **'palimpsest'** like a richly illuminated, medieval manuscript with words and writing added over the centuries. So, this landscape can be 'read' like a manuscript, and in some cases, may take us back for several thousand years and often at least several centuries. The timeline of people and nature is unique, unrepeatable and irreplaceable.

Whitwell Wood, Derbyshire, winter 2023

Because these sites have historically been protected and worked as 'woods' they contain evidence of human history and activities going back centuries or thousands of years and which has mostly been lost from the surrounding countryside or from urban landscapes. The remarkable biodiversity of the ancient woods is a direct result of the land-use timeline.

From the 1950s onwards, forestry has been increasingly mechanised although even in the 1960s and 1970s it was largely by men and chainsaws. Since that time, work has increasingly been done by a very few itinerant workers with little connection to a specific site over time. This situation has developed to the point today that huge machines and a handful of workers cut, process, and extract timber and then depart the site for their next designation. The machines are working the woods but they, in just a few hours, erase all that went before with deep track-marks and skids gouging deep into the earth and in heritage and archaeology. The ecology is also compromised but may often recover – at least in part. The archaeology is destroyed. Taking the manuscript analogy, the medieval parchment is now replaced by a cheap paperback novel......

What do the big machines and timber dragging do:

- They physically erase the ground surface – which means removal of much of the archaeology going back centuries.

- They displace earth-fast stones and boulders – ancient archaeology.

- They damage and remove vegetation but also cause massive release of nutrients through the disruption of these low-nutrient soils which impacts on ecology going forwards. This is rarely considered but the disturbance triggers nutrient-driven ecological succession resulting in invasive colonisers such as bramble. This will change and shade-out the unique ancient woodland flora.

- Not only does this modern, industrial management remove the patina of antiquity, but it imposes new marks and scars that disguise those from earlier centuries. [The felt-tip pen on the Mona Lisa].

- New access roads and even lorry turning circles are created destroying ancient woodland features such as wood-banks etc.

- Soils are disrupted and this leads to massive erosion and loss to the woodland system of nutrients for future tree growth.

- Erosion carries soil and organic materials downslope during storm events causing downstream pollution as well as long-term impoverishment of the woodland soils.

- Major disruption causes carbon release to the atmosphere exacerbating climate change.

- Impact on trees, vegetation and soils exacerbates runoff during storm events to massively increase downstream flooding and also water pollution.

Vehicle tracks in Whitwell Wood, Derbyshire, 2020

**[This is what I call 'doodling on the Mona Lisa'
– still a painting, but not what it was].**

Unrecognised impacts

So far, little has been said about deep-soil and surface impacts through vehicle compaction effects. This has been shown by the Environment Agency to be a causative factor in major flooding events because heavy machines on farmland since the 1950s have led to soil pans of compressed earth below the soil surface. This means that water fails to percolate through resulting in a lack of vital recharge of water aquifers and hugely increased runoff during storm events. It is probable that the same things happen in woodlands where big machines are used and the surface becomes hardened and compacted, with deep-soil compaction compounding the effects. With increasingly extreme storm events, which are becoming more frequent, this makes downstream flooding much worse.

But there is more, because most mature or ancient trees are surprisingly shallow-rooted, and their roots spread a considerable distance out from the trunk at about ground level. The compaction described is therefore hugely damaging to the trees and, combined with nutrient release already described, detrimental to vital mycorrhizal fungi. Thus, the trees' natural defence systems to combat diseases are compromised. Furthermore, since much of the current management is driven by disease control orders, all the issues described above, will, I suggest, make the woods and trees more vulnerable to outbreaks of pests and diseases.

Finally, and perhaps a topic for a future note, the recent history of mono-culture plantations into ancient woodland sites, and often with exotic tree species, is surely one of the drivers behind current problems of pests and diseases. This is of course along with the stresses of atmospheric fallout of nitrogen affecting tree mycorrhizas, of global environmental changes, of globalisation, and of urbanisation. The knee-jerk response of felling and removal simply cannot resolve these issues.

Heritage and woodland management

Some years ago, in a discussion about vehicle damage to the archaeology of an ancient woodland on a long-term lease to the Forestry Commission and managed by them, the FC archaeologist of the time stated, '*Even ancient woods have to pay for themselves ......*'. This was followed by the comments, '*Well they only went through the monument twice....*', and '*It's just a few medieval charcoal hearths and we have got plenty of those.....*'.

More recently, responding to an enquiry from a member of the public about damage to an ancient wood by timber extraction vehicles, a spokesperson for Natural England said, that they did not take heritage aspects into account in the management of woodland Sites of Special Scientific Interest.

The actual statement was. '*I appreciate your concerns about the potential impact to the archaeological interest at ******** but SSSI consent granted by Natural England* *can only take account of the likely impact of proposed works on the SSSI notified interest and doesn't consider the historic interest of a given site.'* In other words, in an 'ancient wood' so designated because of its land-use history and timeline, this is not considered when evaluating work on the ground. Such a protocol does not seem to be acceptable.

One comment from a forestry manager at a site meeting to discuss practice and impacts, was that these were, historically, working woods and all they were doing was 'working them' today. Furthermore, if the heritage and archaeology have been removed by land management beyond the woodland boundary, then why does it matter within the wood? Essentially, if destruction has been accepted outside the woodland, then why should it be curtailed within the wood? Of course, the answer to the latter is that these sites are even more precious because they are often all that now remains and that is under threat of imminent destruction through contemporary management.

Impacts on PAWS [Planted Ancient Woodland Sites]

The discussion at the 2024 Sheffield meeting raised an interesting point, if PAWS woodlands are impoverished in heritage features due to re-planting in the 1950s-1970s period – 'The First Locust Years'- then what does this tell us about process and impacts? If this was the effect of planting with relatively small machines and a lot of manpower, – i.e., the erasing of heritage value - then that is hardly an indictment of the process. Modern extraction and re-planting involve far bigger machines and much heavier ground-impact.

Of course, as already explained, PAWS sites can still have heritage [archaeological / ecological] interest, but they are often somewhat compromised. The worst forestry impacts on historic landscapes were probably deep-ploughing on peat soils which affected heritage, ecology, drainage, floodwater runoff, and of course carbon release. Also, of relevance is that many forestry sites not on woodlands (but perhaps on heath, moor, or unimproved pasture) also had irreplaceable heritage features and many were irreparably damaged. Simply being a 'forestry' site does not necessarily mean there is nothing of value in the landscape.

There is clearly a lack of awareness. But also, there are the impacts of local authority service cuts on support such as by local archaeological services which in many cases simply do not function at the level required. Also, if they do, then there is little guarantee that they will have necessary records in the system for 'woodland' heritage, or even that the officers themselves will effectively recognise this. A conclusion might be that even where there are checks and balances with regard to management causing site damage, they are simply ineffective.

How current woodland management triggered the 'New Locust Years' for woodland history & heritage

The heritage and archaeological interest associated with ancient woods are uniquely interesting, informative, and important, yet at the same time, incredibly vulnerable. Often the result of long-term timeline continuity, the heritage features include soils and sediments, earth-fast stones, banks and ditches, boundaries, trackways, pits, and platforms, and both living biota and worked trees. Many key features are difficult to recognise and record and are easily disrupted or damaged. Furthermore, modern forestry work with ever-bigger vehicles may gouge deep tracks and marks into the landscape which both erase historic features and also impose new ones to overlay and blur the ancient heritage. The historic marks represent what Rackham described as a 'palimpsest' with a record of human presence in layers each embedded over the earlier periods and adding to them but not eroding what went before. In *traditionally-managed ancient woods*, the overlain marks of history along with ecology and worked trees, can be read like the pages of a book. It is this historical record including the associated ecology, that modern, contemporary management with big machines erases from the countryside and which cannot be restored. Each timeline of a site in the landscape is unique and any damage is permanent and irreparable. For this reason, heavy mechanical interventions on site destroy the inherent '*ancient*' character of a wood and convert it from 'ancient woodland' (as defined by Peterken and

Rackham), and into something different. Such sites are no longer the result of traditional management but are *'industrially-managed woodlands'*. It is still woodland but is now degraded and in extreme cases might be considered *'post-industrial'*.

One major transformation was with the advent of modern 'forestry' (in the 1800s and 1900s), different and distinctive from traditional 'woodmanship' (that persisted from the time of Domesday to the mid-1950s). Production of cycles of native timber and underwood were replaced by largely exotic timbers. Throughout the twentieth century the impact of increasingly mechanised systems was to transform entirely the processes and products of modern 'forestry' with two world wars providing political and financial impetus. During the 1960s and subsequently, lip-service was paid to delivery of wider benefits such as Forest Parks, but the underlying principles were increasingly intensive timber products and mostly with planted exotic species.

The outcomes of the modern approach

Oliver Rackham described Britain in the 1950s and 1960s as the *'**Locust Years**'* of modern forestry. During this time of the post-war forestry and farming boom, untold damage was done to ancient woodlands which had remained relatively intact for nearly a thousand years. This period was driven by the socio-economic forces of post-Depression, and post-war periods, and the opportunities provided by new technology and increased mechanisation. Even now however, most work was by men with chainsaws and relatively small tractors. Forestry was even promoted to boost rural employment which would certainly not be the case today.

There was then a change in approach during the 1980s and 1990s, as the ideas of Rackham and his contemporaries seemed to change hearts and minds in terms of conservation and woodland management as opposed to forestry. However, during the same period approaches employing people to work the forest manually morphed into huge, heavy machines often operated by a single person. The impacts increased in parallel to these changes, and now this modernised 'efficient' forestry has re-emerged and extends from productive 'forests' to 'conservation' sites too.

The consequences of such modern interventions include:

1) Damage to heritage / archaeology – both *in* the woods and *of* the woods.

2) Loss or compromise of ancient woodland features.

3) Cessation of ancient woodland timelines.

4) Damage to the woodland biota especially ground flora – with long-term trajectory shifts and successions associated with disturbance and nutrient release.

5) Damage to tree roots and mycorrhizal associations through compression.

6) Damage to formerly 'worked' trees and 'retired veterans'.

7) Damage to soil structure through compaction and increased floodwater runoff.

8) Soil erosion and consequent downstream pollution of watercourses and loss to the atmosphere of carbon released from the disrupted soil profile.

9) Damage to ancient access routes / footpaths etc.

10) Damage to landscape and aesthetics.

11) Local 'cultural severance' from the community.

12) Reduced climate change resilience.

13) Reduced health and wellbeing benefits for local people.

The New Locust Years

The damage of this new wave of modern, intensive, heavy-duty forestry is rarely questioned and the adverse impacts described above are mostly unseen. Many projects are even overseen by managers with only limited experience of practical forestry operations and not effectively briefed on woodland history, ecology, or heritage. Additionally, they have little in-house guidance or support on these matters. Furthermore, current financial constraints placed on local government, agencies, and charitable conservation bodies frequently mean limited access to appropriate advisory services and expertise. This is not a recipe for sensitive and effective conservation management.

Vehicle tracks through Whitwell Wood, Derbyshire, 2023

Chapter 4: Some tangible examples of site-based issues

Case study examples of sites damaged or destroyed by insensitive management interventions are documented in some of the readings suggested in the bibliography.

Case-studies of woodland management & heritage issues

Six site-based case-studies are presented from the three regions of the English Midlands (South Yorkshire, North Derbyshire, and North Nottinghamshire). Some of these were previously discussed by Rotherham (2021b and 2024b).

It is worth noting that these site studies all document irreparable damage to ancient woodland heritage, with in part at least, the conversion of 'traditionally-managed ancient woods' to 'industrially-managed ancient woodland sites' (or 'post-industrial woods'). However, in all cases those responsible for the works felt they were doing a good job and indeed, were passionate about 'woodland conservation'. They certainly did not intend to cause damage although in some cases, the over-riding pressure was the serving of Statutory Plant Health Notices which meant urgent by-passing of any agreed plans or conservation processes.

Case-study 1. Greno Wood, Sheffield (SK33 95):

At Greno Woods to the north of Sheffield, a major woodland management project funded by the national

Heritage Lottery Fund was well underway before any historic landscape and archaeological survey was undertaken. One result of the premature management interventions was the destruction of an important grouping of early industrial charcoal hearths which had previously been notified to the nature conservation NGO that owned and managed the large complex of woods.

Here we have a major, publicly-funded programme of woodland management undertaken with 'Heritage' Lottery money but without prior survey and with no approved management plan. Problems identified were (a) the timeline of the funding for the management, and (b) that there was no money for doing necessary surveys, for producing a management plan, or for consulting on the same. With these omissions, the work went ahead anyway and caused significant damage to the site's cultural heritage. Retrospectively, funding was obtained to undertake archaeological surveys but again, with surveyors inexperienced in woodland work, much was simply misidentified and wrongly attributed. Wood-drying kilns known as Q-pits (Jones, 2009) for example, were noted as stone-getting pits (Mel Jones pers. comm.). In the 93-page management plan the archaeological findings merited less than two pages and included a statement to the effect that '400 other archaeological features' were found ranging in scale from the (possible) remains of a fortified medieval hall to, 'a vast array of quarry holes, walls and features associated with the woodlands working past'. Many of the so-called quarry holes were various pits and platforms from charcoal and whitecoal production (Mel Jones pers. comm.). Significant veteran trees such as coppices and clones were again overlooked and as noted, industrial charcoal-manufacturing sites were unrecognised and unrecorded. Archaeological surveys (rather than woodland heritage surveys) were undertaken in 2013-2014 and a management plan was produced in 2015. However, active site management had already begun prior to this and caused significant, irreparable, and avoidable damage to both ecology and to cultural heritage.

Typical charcoal-burner's shelter, Sheffield but not Greno Wood, late 1800s

Charcoal burn early 1900s, not Greno Wood

Case-study 2. Whitwell Wood, North Derbyshire (SK52 78):

Danger forestry work, Whitwell Wood, Derbyshire

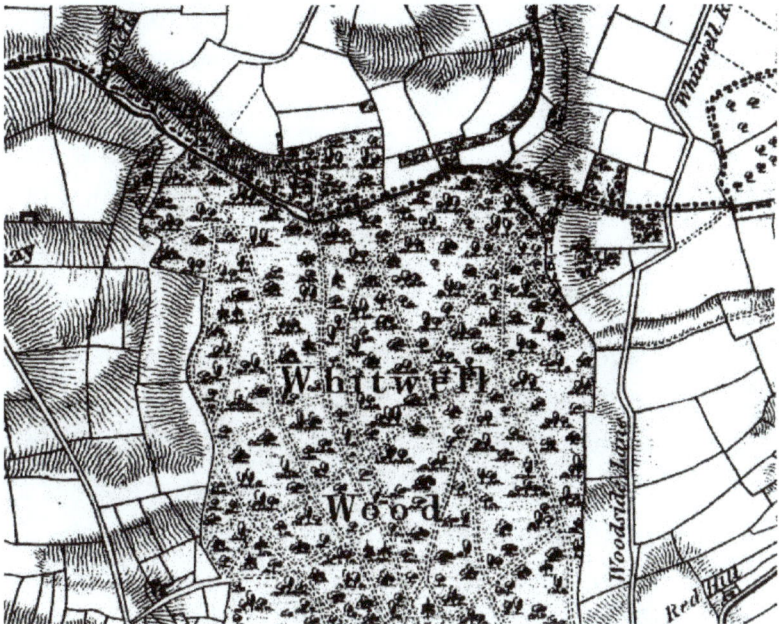

Whitwell Wood, Derbyshire, early 1800s

Another case-study has been researched in some detail at Whitwell Wood in North Derbyshire. This is part of the privately-owned Portland estate (Welbeck Abbey) but on a long-term lease to the Forestry Commission. This large woodland is situated on magnesian limestone rocks with alkaline soils and hence a rich ecology. However, in the period of timber crisis during and following World War One, most of the site was clear-felled and then re-planted with an experimental mix of exotic conifers, sycamore (*Acer pseudoplatanus*), beech (*Fagus sylvatica*), and some oak (*Quercus robur*). This re-planting was done manually and therefore with only limited disruption to the historic landscape features throughout the site. The wood has numerous pits and platforms associated with industrial charcoal manufacture, and both banks and ditches. There are trackways associated with woodland management at that time (from the 1920s to the 1970s). Some archaeological surveys have been done of the main upstanding features, but these have yet to be fully evaluated in-depth or incorporated into a coherent management plan for consultation.

However, the key feature of the site is an extensive bank and ditch system with two major enclosures of unknown provenance located close-by a major routeway (north-south) through the wood. There are what appear to be east-west orientated cultivation lynchets on the adjacent north-facing slope. Other parts of the wood have extensive zones of medieval ridge-and-furrow field systems, and there are sections of drystone walls. The wood has sites close to the bank-and-ditch feature which have been identified as early buildings with post-holes, and there are numerous barrows and cairns throughout the site. An informal visit to the site with a highly experienced archaeologist familiar with the area, suggested that the site is of a least regional and possibly national significance, but yet to be effectively assessed, designated, and protected.

Indeed, none of this eco-cultural landscape has been effectively surveyed or evaluated in terms of a landscape-scale consideration of the heritage and archaeology both in the wood and of the wood. This is despite the wood being in an on-going programme of publicly-funded major thinning and timber removal works. The current on-going management involves heavy machinery gouging through the earthworks to a depth of a metre or more and cutting swathes several metres across.

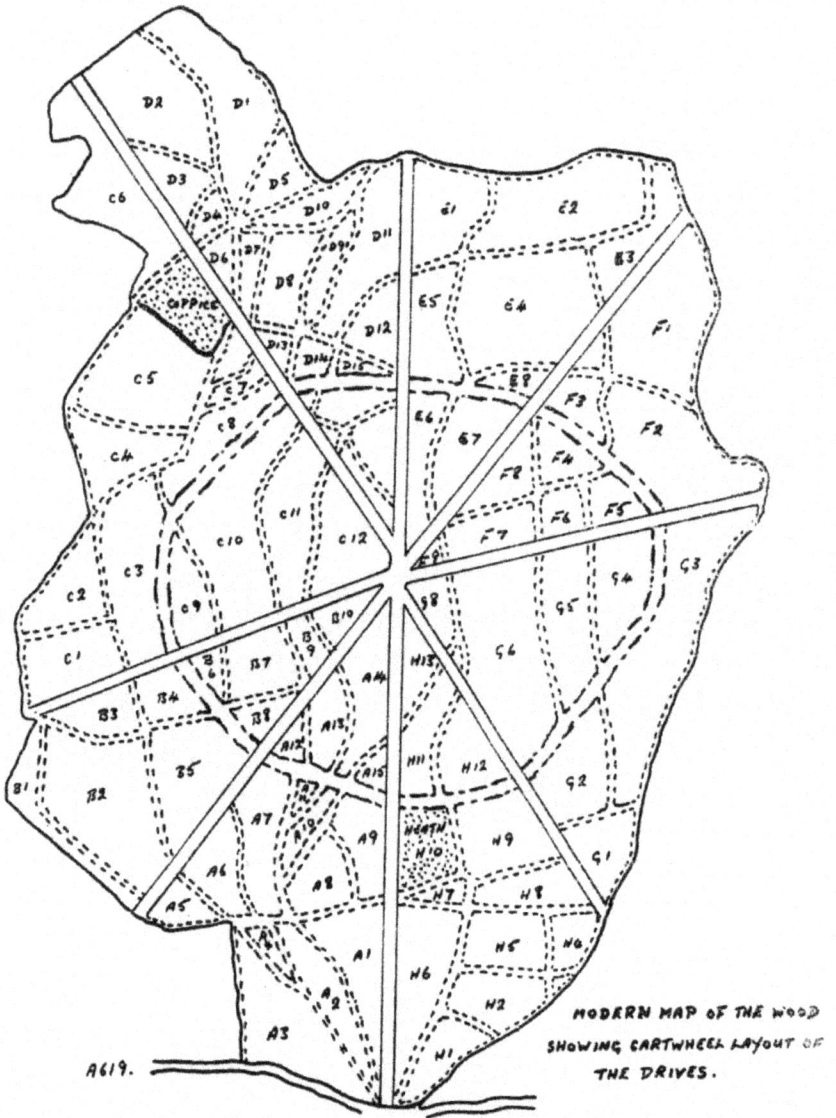

MODERN MAP OF THE WOOD
SHOWING CARTWHEEL LAYOUT OF
THE DRIVES.

Whitwell Wood, Derbyshire, 1980s

The works have major adverse impacts on public access too with no apparent reference to good practice in terms of leaving footpaths passable. Rutted, wet, tracks littered with tree debris are left on site for months after work has finished. Each time the site work is undertaken there is massive and destructive impact on the cultural heritage landscape. Furthermore, when initial complaints were made to the Forestry Commission the response from their national archaeological advisor was that the damage was acceptable and necessary for the timber management work, which we were also told was loss-making anyway. Subsequently, a meeting was held on-site with the lead Forestry Commission officer responsible for the area and this led to an undertaking not to repeat the damage in future operations, and to commission appropriate awareness-raising training for his staff. The latter never happened, and the damage continues to this day, some seventeen years later.

Whitwell Wood, Derbyshire impacts of woodland management

In practice, connected in part to government financial cuts to the agency and on-going reorganisation, neither of these actions happened. The site work and associated damage continue annually to cause serious attrition to the heritage resource. A reason given for the problems was that because of government regulations the Forestry Commission was now obligated to pass its implementation works to private contractors. This meant a number of issues arose which they were aware of but could not resolve. Firstly, there was little opportunity to train operatives in recognising heritage features or in low-impact working. Secondly, there was a major barrier to halting works during a wet period in winter or early spring (i.e., when conditions were unsuitable) because it now involved cancelling or delaying a contract and therefore an additional cost. Finally, the Commission now had little in-house ability to oversee heritage aspects of contacted works. Additionally, there was no baseline survey of archaeology and heritage from which to work and no agreed management plan. There is also significant disagreement between experts in terms of the interpretation of the site features.

Public information Whitwell Wood, 2020

83

Whitwell Wood Natural History Group with a demonstration charcoal burn, 1980s

Interestingly at Whitwell in the 1990s, a local community group (Whitwell Wood Natural History Group) was established to study and protect the site. This local society developed pioneering approaches to re-coppicing areas for conservation, the cutting of scalloped edges to major rides, and the construction of modern interpretations of prehistoric or medieval shelters. They also undertook demonstrations of traditional charcoal burning with workers living rough on-site for several weeks at a time. This was interpretative community archaeology well ahead of its time and which has now been lost.

Although there have been several significant surveys of archaeology over the period since the 1980s, the site remains incompletely known in terms of both its archaeology and its ecology, though it is well used for recreational access. The main shortfall is the absence of an agreed and publicly consulted management plan with guidance for site forestry works. In particular the attempts at mitigation of vehicle impacts are ineffective. Furthermore, inspection of the known archaeology as mapped, albeit incompletely, indicates that should the Rackham recommendations be followed, there should be no vehicle access off the drives. In this case too, since the demise of the local group presence on site, there is no effective stakeholder engagement, and the resource diminishes year on year.

A meeting with the Commission officers and other interested stakeholders from the local authority was held in 2023, but again there was a disparity between what the officers felt was acceptable practice and damage on site and the conservation viewpoint. A key issue that was raised and unresolved was that the 'monuments' that were recognised were the visibly obvious upstanding features. That these were major structures criss-crossing the wood over hundreds of metres had not protected them from machine-damage, although in recent years, they had been marked up prior to operations on-site. However, deep cuts still occurred as close as five metres to major enclosures, and there was a lack of recognition of the heritage nature of the connecting landscape and not just individual, visible 'monuments'.

Along with these observations, the matter of damage to woodland heritage such as medieval trackways, platforms and pits, banks and ditches, and worked trees, was raised. This includes unmapped medieval charcoal production hearths badly compromised. The only response from the Commission officers was to request that these be mapped and reported to the site manager – but without any funding or support for this to be done. This is a large site, and the task would amount to somewhere between four and six weeks work.

Case-study 3. Hardwick Wood, Clumber Park, Nottinghamshire (SK63 76):

A little further south of Whitwell is Clumber Park in Nottinghamshire, the one-time grand home of the Dukes of Newcastle. Now a National Trust property, the site was part of the great royal forest of Sherwood, then enclosed as a landscape park, but abandoned and sold in the 1930s and 1940s. Following local protests and public subscription, the site was purchased for conservation and amenity by the fledgling National Trust.

The urgency of the purchase was in part to prevent a local woodyard from acquiring the site in order to fell the great veteran oak trees of Hardwick Wood, one of a number of ancient woods on the site. However, having bought Clumber, the response of the National Trust at the time was to fell the oaks anyway to help recoup their financial outlay. The evidence remains to this day with great stumps rotting in the ground in the wood where just a handful of great oaks now remain. The scenario and approach resonates with Oliver Rackham's observations at another historic treescape managed by the National Trust, at Hatfield Forest in Essex (Rackham, 1989). Again, as with case at Whitwell, there has been no comprehensive ecological survey of the site and absolutely no assessment of woodland archaeology and heritage. The area is ancient woodland and has numerous woodbanks and ditches, culturally-significant trees, charcoal hearths, pits, and other features. Furthermore, the wood has abundant evidence of Second World War occupation when it was used for military training and as a transient stage for tank transportation. On the one hand this intensive use compromised the earlier archaeology but on the other hand it left a legacy of wartime heritage which itself is now recognised as 'archaeology'.

In recent years however, the Trust undertook major removal of both invasive rhododendron (*Rhododendron ponticum*) and of timber. Some of this timber extraction was of planted exotic conifers but other works were felling of miscellaneous mature and semi-mature deciduous trees. There are complications with the complexity of this site but also that it is on a friable sandy soil derived from the underlying sandstone rock.

One of the few remaining veteran oaks at Hardwick Wood, Clumber Park, Nottinghamshire

This means that the woodland archaeology such as banks, ditches, platforms, and trackways naturally degrades rather quickly and therefore less obvious than in other situations. Nevertheless, there are areas within the park which have extensive and rich heritage of earthworks. Worse still, the remaining upstanding features are very easily and significantly compromised by site work with heavy machinery as was the case here. Once again, there was no prior survey of woodland archaeology and eco-cultural heritage and there is no agreed management plan that has been commented on by stakeholders. In this vulnerable but important landscape, considerable damage has been done to the archaeological resource. Sadly, much of this work was undertaken in the name at least, of conservation, and the damage was unintentional.

Small-leaved lime lapsed coppice now stumped at Clumber Park, Nottinghamshire

Case-study 4. Moss Valley Woods, North Derbyshire (SK37 80):

Whinacre Wood, Moss Valley, North Derbyshire

The fourth case-study is from the Moss Valley in North Derbyshire. Here a complex of woods owned by Sheffield City Council and the Woodland Trust is now managed in part by the Wildlife Trust and in part by the Woodland Trust. In the 1980s, the Sheffield City Council estate was proposed for grant-aided coniferisation but intervention by the author prevented that, and the group of several ancient woods became a nature reserve. Half of one major wood was privately owned and following hugely destructive machine harvesting with public grant-aid, was sold to an independent conservation group. Another major block of woods was owned by the private Renishaw estate, and they sold this to the Woodland

Trust. The deciduous woodland had received planting grants for conifers in the 1960s and 1970s, and the Trust wished to remove these. Accordingly, a review of woodland archaeology was commissioned, and a 'safe' low-impact extraction programme was both planned and implemented (Rotherham, & Avison, 1997, 1998). The work here involved 'snigging' which is the removal of timber by heavy horses. Pre-planned exit routes helped avoid damage to archaeological and heritage features. Ancient coppice stools were identified and left intact, with hearths, pits, platforms, banks, ditches, and routeways largely avoided. The additional works necessary were generously funded by a private sponsor of the Woodland Trust charity and at this stage the programme was taken as an example of good practice. The survey works even here were relatively superficial and many features were simply noted as 'sensitive' and to be protected but not fully identified to type or period. This was of course before GPS, LiDAR, and GIS were available.

Other areas of these ancient woodlands are subject to on-going works with major periods of tree felling though not of timber removal. Historically, these sites were former coppice woods with extensive charcoal and whitecoal (kiln-dried wood) manufacture but abandoned in the Victorian period and re-planted in the late 1800s and early 1900s with mainly oak, beech, and sweet chestnut (*Castanea sativa*). Neither of the latter two species is native here.

Other areas of these ancient woodlands are subject to on-going works with major periods of tree felling though not of timber removal. Historically, these sites were former coppice woods with extensive charcoal and whitecoal (kiln-dried wood) manufacture but abandoned in the Victorian period and re-planted in the late 1800s and early 1900s with mainly oak, beech, and sweet chestnut (*Castanea sativa*). Neither of the latter two species is native here.

Metal slag from medieval smelting site, Whinacre Wood, Derbyshire

Linear feature in Whinacre Wood, Moss Valley. Early industrial or medieval

On the woods they manage here, the Wildlife Trust commissioned surveys of archaeological features though not by specialists in 'woodland archaeology' and heritage. This problem has already been commented on, and essentially the surveyors missed or misinterpreted much of the heritage. Furthermore, the site management was undertaken with little evidence of it being informed by knowledge of eco-cultural heritage. Considerable significant damage was once again done inadvertently. This was again in part because tree removal was driven largely by arboricultural considerations (as opposed to 'woodland' management) with no recognition of culturally-significant trees such as re-grown coppice. Trackways, charcoal hearths, and associated processing areas were all adversely affected and discussion with contractors on site confirmed that they had not been briefed on any aspects of landscape sensitivity. Whilst there had been a walkover archaeological survey and there was a current management plan (Doar, 2016) which stated that archaeological features would be protected, in practice that was not the case. In a new phase of operations considerable positive progress was made, in principle at least, to work more sensitively and to reduce levels of heritage damage.

Footings of an old boundary wall, Whinacre Wood, Moss Valley, North Derbyshire

Similar operations have also occurred in the adjacent woods managed by the Woodland Trust, and which also has complex groupings of early industrial charcoal hearths, trackways, processing areas, metal smelting sites, and probably earlier archaeology too. Management has clearly been driven by ecological targets and the application of standard silvicultural practice but without any consideration of the eco-cultural landscape and heritage. There is a management plan (Anon., 2018b) but again, this does not translate into heritage conservation on the ground and considerable damage occurred during the current phase of management. This situation was made hugely worse by disease-control removal of European larch (*Larix decidua*) in 2020 – 2021 with

95

associated massive disruption to both the ecology and the archaeology of the sites. This included the removal of a significant section of medieval wood-bank, and the creation of a large turning circle for timber extraction lorries within the medieval wood. Some site assessment was undertaken by university academics but without specialist knowledge of woodland heritage or site management, and very obvious charcoal heaths, Q-pits, trackways, and other features were overlooked, and many have been compromised. Again, discussions and site meetings followed, and recommendations were made and in principle agreed. Some of these are now underway to resolve issues, but such heritage damage cannot be undone. Fortunately, in the recent period of disease-control intervention, some of the most sensitive areas avoided the worst damage but earlier works to supposedly rejuvenate the woodland resulted in the annihilation of several major, medieval hearths. As already noted elsewhere, because these were never adequately surveyed, we don't even know what has been lost and a key part of the story of these woods has been erased from the site and from memory. Evidence of the scale of damage is indicated by extensive wash-off of charcoal across a wide swathe of the lower slopes of the steeply-sloping woodland.

Extraction tracks through a medieval charcoal hearth adjacent to a major Q-pit, Whinacre Wood, Derbyshire - disrupted charcoal washed downslope

Deep vehicle extraction tracks through a medieval charcoal hearth adjacent to a major Q-pit, Whinacre Wood, Derbyshire. Auger provides scale

Vehicle tracks and washed out charcoal, Whinacre Wood, Derbyshire

Lorry turning circle that obliterated the medieval wood-bank at Whinacre Wood, Derbyshire

Section of medieval wood-bank, Whinacre Wood, Derbyshire

Case-study 5. Rough Standhills, Whirlow, Sheffield (SK2983):

This large woodland recognised by Natural England in part as both 'ancient woodland' and 'ancient wood-pasture' was subject to a preliminary walkover by the author prior to site work beginning. Indeed, the owner (Sheffield City Council) had previously identified this area as requiring woodland archaeological assessment prior to any site works. For reasons unknown, but probably a mix of limited budget for necessary work and the pressure of a Defra order to undertaken radical clearance of diseased larches, the clearance ultimately occurred without survey, assessment, or conservation guidance. Worse still as a compounding factor, the use of heavy machinery on-site was during an especially wet spring. (A similar situation had previously exacerbated problems at Whitwell for example). An offer to walk on site in order to brief the woodland managers before work began was rejected as 'they knew what they were doing'. However, the consequent impact of the works was catastrophic and caused major and significant damage to unrecorded eco-cultural heritage.

Two years later, major downslope flooding and soil erosion have been reported as a consequence of the operations.

Rough Standhills, Sheffield, devastated by clearance

This was a mix of PAWS woodland, and ancient wood-pasture, and following machine extraction of timber the site was left resembling a World War One battlefield with charcoal from the damaged medieval hearths washing off downslope. Some mature oaks were left and these inadvertently safeguarded (fortuitously), some heritage features including Q-pits. [Interestingly, an informal survey visit around a quarter of a mile away, downslope, has since revealed major Iron Age and Neolithic archaeological features previously unknown. This was reported at the 2024, Sheffield conference. Historically part of the same medieval wood-pasture countryside, it is likely that Rough Standhills held similar heritage features now lost].

The management undoubtedly caused massive loss of carbon to the atmosphere, significant soil erosion and pollution of the nearby watercourse, destruction of heritage and of woodland ecology with long-term changes to vegetation due to disturbance, nutrient release and soil loss. It is reported that properties downhill now suffer from flooding due to the altered hydrology of the site, and the ornamental ponds in the amenity park at Whirlowbrook are filling with silt. Ironically, the valley-wide area is an exemplar of 'slowing the flow naturally' to reduce downstream risk of flooding in this flood-prone catchment.

The year after work was complete a community tree-planting took place, which on sites of this sort is unnecessary as trees will come back quickly through natural regeneration, and that has been the case here. Indeed, many of the planted trees failed the following year during a severe drought and others were eaten by deer. The main positive result of the tree-planting was probably just community involvement rather than woodland creation. Development of the secondary 'natural 'woodland will occur in sites such as this and planting is not required. The resulting woodland will have ecological attributes of secondary, spontaneous woodland and some nature conservation value. However, this is different and distinctive from that of ancient woodland and the heritage has on the one hand been erased, and on the other masked by the modern impacts. This was another site problem triggered by a Statutory Plant Health Notices and the desire 'to do something' and pressure to 'act now'.

Case-study 6. Wyming Brook SSSI and Local Nature Reserve, Rivelin Valley, Sheffield (SK27 87):

Another Statutory Plant Health Notice site associated with Common Larch affected by *Phytophthora* infection in the vicinity, was served for this regionally important site. Wyming Brook is a complex site being ancient woodland (wood-pasture historically) and with known heritage including medieval trackways, ancient, worked rowans, holly clones, medieval charcoal heaths, and more, but little of this thoroughly surveyed or documented. However, there is a further element with site being acquired and planted by the then landowner as an ornamental driveway with Corsican Pine, European Larch, and Sweet Chestnut especially, prominent in the landscape. On account of the site's cultural assets and associated wildlife interest including many uncommon bird species dependent on the now mature larches, the area was one of the region's most popular countryside recreational sites. Notable birds utilising the site have included numbers of common crossbills, parrot crossbills, siskins, lesser redpolls, goldcrests, and many more, including birds of prey nesting in the tall conifers. In the 1990s, the site was identified by the present author as one of Sheffield's twelve proposed Local Nature Reserves and subsequently passed on a long-term lease to the Sheffield and Rotherham Wildlife Trust.

The problems in this case, were the impact of the Plant Health Notice and subsequent issues in terms of process and procedure. Any surveys of heritage and archaeology were essentially desktop reviews of a site lacking field survey and hence showed very little except around the periphery of the wood. Because of limited staff resources by the South Yorkshire Archaeological Service there was no site survey mandated for heritage (similar to the situation with Rough Standhills, above). Despite this being an amenity and conservation woodland and not in any way a commercial forest, the notice was still served and acted upon. It was disputed as to whether or not this site came within the scope of the directive, but this went unchallenged. A site meeting with managers was held and the evidence of significant heritage interest was identified to them by local stakeholders. It was then requested by the managers that a survey and report be undertaken free of charge, which clearly is unreasonable and unrealistic. The features identified from a walkover viewing prior to the field meeting included major medieval charcoal platforms, associated trackways and processing platforms, and culturally-significant veteran trees.

Ancient rowan at Wyming Brook nature reserve, Sheffield

It was noted that the timber felling and extraction would be very expensive and loss-making (though there was reluctance to share the details of costs or the sources of funding – even though these should be in the public domain and transparent). Furthermore, the main cost was in the dragging of timber off-site to be collected by lorry at the roadside. If the trees needed to be killed and / or felled for disease control purposes, but extraction is expensive, then it was suggested that they could simply be ring-barked or felled and dropped to be left on site as deadwood habitat. This would reduce carbon release though soil erosion and degradation, retain carbon in the felled timber, enhance floodwater retention, improve biodiversity, and lessen damage to heritage and to visual amenity. This option was not taken.

Work was eventually undertaken without acceptable heritage surveys or guidance, and there has been no post-operation assessment of damage to heritage or to visual amenity. In terms of public relations, the operations were presented to the public as 'the only option' and something that 'must be done'. There was no challenge to the imposition of the order, or the major costs involved, and no public information on budgets and funding (despite requests for information). The operator's website also stated (incorrectly) that the work would capture carbon and slow the flow of floodwater, which quite clearly it did not. Once again, the officers involved were passionately doing their job but simply misinformed about aspects of eco-cultural heritage, archaeology, and to some extent, the options available. The absence of appropriately qualified expert guidance or publicly consulted proposals served to compound the issues.

European larch at Wyming Brook nature reserve, Sheffield

Some observations from the case-studies

A general observation of the case-studies but also of many other ancient woods now in contemporary management, is that they have emerged in the early twenty-first century as 'leisurely landscapes'. The management of these sites is then increasingly driven by assumptions and aspirations for nature conservation but with a reality of modern-day 'parkification' to accommodate ever-increasing recreational usage. Footpaths are improved and 'dangerous' trees are felled but from a conservation viewpoint this is often inappropriate and unnecessary. Gradually, sites morph from relict medieval and industrial woods into public parks or degraded woods; a situation which becomes more blurred as conservation bodies merge into leisure

106

visit providers. The conservation role of these environmental champion organisations can thus be compromised, and in any case, they often struggle to address matters of eco-cultural heritage and history. In terms of the practicalities of site management by a forestry operative, conservation officers are frequently quite inexperienced.

The availability of best practice guidance is is also problematic, and this is discussed in some depth along with recommendations. However, even when there are funded programmes of woodland restoration research their recommendations can be disastrous for heritage. Take for example, the Europe-wide COST study on coppice wood management presented at the 2017 IUFRO congress in Freiburg. This recommended heavy industrial extraction of coppice from ancient woods and forests. There was no mention at all of history, heritage, or archaeological sensitivity in either the presentation or in the associated project report (Anon., 2017b). The scale of damage to the cultural heritage was catastrophic.

From the case-studies, it is absolutely clear that the problems reported are not unusual but indeed, are becoming the norm. Furthermore, that this is a nationwide issue is confirmed by reports from across the United Kingdom of similar experiences and with almost always, a very unsupportive response from agencies, local authorities, and even conservation NGOs. The scale of the impacts and the consequent losses of genuinely ancient woodland sites is catastrophic and presents huge challenges for future conservation. That this is a problem not merely for heritage but also for long-term ecologies is not widely recognised, and by the time that it is, it may be too late to act.

One of the enclosures, Whitwell Wood, Derbyshire

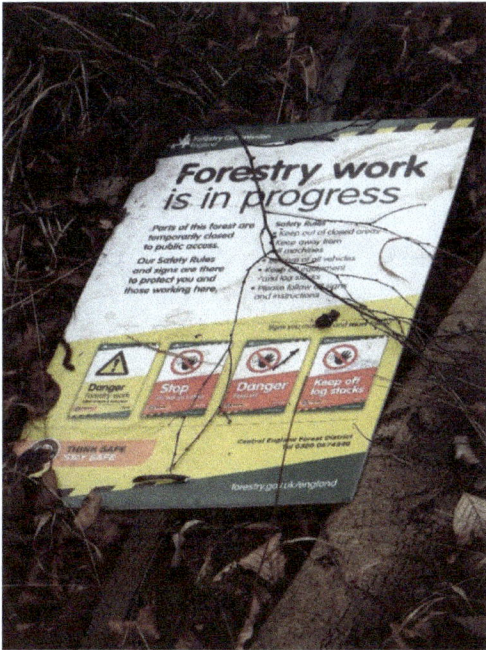

Forestry sign from Whitwell Wood, Derbyshire

Timber at Whitwell Wood, Derbyshire

The worked woodland at Whitwell Wood, 2023

Extracts from technical reports on Whitwell Wood:

These are shown in order to give a flavour of the heritage riches of the site, which is still only incompletely known or understood. Significant heritage trees and botanical indictor plants are omitted but so too are many prehistoric features and for example, medieval charcoal hearths. However, the take-home message indicated clearly by the plans, is that the entire land surface o is a palimpsest of historic features and associated ecology and cannot be managed are a plot of separate 'monuments'. That approach simply fails to effectively protect and conserve the woodland heritage, and yet this is what is done, leading to absolute failure.

Overview plan of Whitwell Wood archaeology features from Zeffertt (1994). The main enclosure (below) from Beresford (2012) and probably either Iron Age or Dark Ages

A scene of devastation at Rough Standhills, Sheffield following woodland management. (above and below)

The evidence of inappropriate and damaging clearance of veteran trees may persist in the landscape for decades. The oak stumps below are from Hatfield Forest in Essex, where the mid-twentieth-century management by the National Trust was severely criticised by Oliver

Rackham. Similar evidence cover Hardwick Wood at National Trust Clumber Park in Nottinghamshire and where the old oaks were 'harvested' in the 1940s to help fund the site acquisition (which was in part to safeguard the old trees!).

Stumps of veteran oaks at Hatfield Forest, in the 2000s and felled in the 1950s (and below)

113

The implications of tree diseases

Several case-study sites were strongly influenced by tree diseases in terms of reports and the serving of statutory notices. In some cases, this process was directly responsible for the subsequent destruction and damage to ancient woods.

Statutory notices and especially the Statutory Plant Health Notice (SPHN) served by Defra and followed up by the Forestry Commission are an understandable reaction to outbreaks of tree diseases. However, many of the control measures clearly do not work and the present way of implementing them is hugely expensive to landowners, local authorities, and conservation organisations, some expending hundreds of thousands of pounds at short notice. Indeed, it seems commonsense that the spread of pests and diseases is almost certainly exacerbated by trauma and stress inflicted on the woodland ecosystems by dramatic, often unplanned interventions. So, not only does this seem to fail in halting the spread but in all probability, it makes things worse, and at great cost.

Most of the financial outlay is not recouped and even with timber sales the operations run at a considerable loss. Observation and action research on case-study sites confirms that there is little or no discussion, minimal advice, and an overall threatening tone to the notification – essentially 'do this or else'.

It is also clear that the current waves of pests and diseases result from massive global stresses such as climate change and extreme weather, atmospheric pollution such as nitrogen fallout, globalisation and associated movement of plants and soils around the world, and other human-induced impacts. The final one to mention is of course the twentieth-century planting of mono-culture commercial woodlands which are just ripe for invasion by pests and diseases.

However, the consequence of all this is much of the bad management described earlier in the book results directly from these control measures. They seem to trump local environmental democracy such as management according to agreed and approved management plans. Radical interventions are applied with minimal site survey or monitoring and irreparable damage is done to heritage, archaeology, ecology and amenity. Site managers hide behind a veneer of misinformation and fall back on the idea that 'we have no choice'. Informed communication with the public stakeholders is minimal. Essentially there is no challenge to the diktat from above.

- **Statutory Plant Health Notices (SPHN):**

  - These are issued by the Forestry Commission / Defra or other plant health authorities if a notifiable tree pest or disease is found at a site.

  - The notice requires owners or managers to take specified actions to attempt to eradicate or contain the pest or disease.

  - The necessary actions may include felling or ring-barking of infected trees or retaining infected material on-site.

  - Failure to respond effectively to an SPHN may trigger enforcement action, prosecution, and a fine.

- **Reporting Tree Pests and Diseases:**

  - Suspected tree pests and diseases can be reported to the Forestry Commission with online reporting tool called 'Tree Alert'. However, many disease outbreaks are identified by remote sensing of the woodland canopy.

- **Some notifiable pests and diseases of UK trees:**
  - European or Japanese Larch affected by *Phytophthora ramorum*
  - Sweet Chestnut affected by *Phytophthora ramorum*
  - Sweet Chestnut affected by Sweet Chestnut Blight (*Cryphonectria parasitica*)
  - Spruce with Spruce Bark Beetle (*Ips typographus*) affecting exotic spruce
  - *Phytophthora pluvialis* - a recent arrival affecting a number of exotic trees
  - Oak Processionary Moth (*Thaumetopoea processionea*)
  - Dutch Elm Disease (*Ophiostoma novo-ulmi*)
  - Acute Oak Decline – maybe caused by bacteria (*Brenneria goodwinii, Gibbsiella quercinecans, Rahnella Victoriana*)
  - Powdery Mildew (several species of fungi including *Erysiphe* species)

Examples of catastrophic damage have included control of ash die-back and of larch *Phytophthora*. Interventions have caused irreparable damage to sites, and in the case of ash die-back have in some cases involved felling or crown-reduction of healthy trees simply affected by a severe drought year and high summertime temperatures.

This means unnecessary damage and also significant expenditure on wasted operations. Furthermore, whereas initial guidance was to fell and remove affected trees, the advice is now to leave them so long as there is no obvious risk or hazard associated with failure. One reason for this is that this strategy allows disease-resistant trees to survive and their genes to flow within the tree population. This makes absolute sense but does mean that the earlier expenditure and environmental damage were unnecessary.

At the end of the process, the irony is that much of this attempted control is in order to preserve trees and woodland, and to (where possible) retain commercial timber value. Yet this work which destroys ecology, heritage, and amenity, is mostly undertaken at a significant financial cost.

Chapter 5: Conclusions & Recommendations - solutions and a way forwards

There is new and improved guidance from Natural England on the selection and designation of 'Ancient Woodland' for the 'Ancient Woodland Inventory' (e.g., Sansum & Bannister, 2018), and this is welcomed since many sites have been lost by being, for various reasons, omitted. [However, a valid criticism might be the lack of wider consultation on the actual document]. Similarly, the Forestry Commission has presented new on-line guidance on woodland archaeology assessment (Anon., 2023) [again not widely consulted on], but much needed and welcomed. However, these are not enough, are insufficiently comprehensive, and are of limited accessibility or use on site. Moreover, the continuing damage to and destruction of, woodland heritage confirms that they have not solved the problem. Furthermore, there is the ongoing complication of the forestry services being split into research and information dissemination, a grant-awarding team for private landowners, the land-owning and managing Forest Enterprise, and different access to or provision of guidance to the different categories of sites. This makes a cohesive approach rather difficult, and most private landowners for example, have limited knowledge or awareness of woodland heritage or its importance and sensitivity. An additional complication is that many local authorities and the Forestry Commission itself, now outreach most site management and which is then subject to contractual obligations. This makes it harder to train site operators to work in the ways as suggested, and there is pressure to carry on allowing work during unsuitable weather conditions such as heavy rain when much catastrophic damage occurs. However, contracts do offer opportunities to specify the necessary compliance but of course, this will cost more money, and the Commission will be reluctant to go down that route.

Following wide discussions with a range of interest groups and stakeholders it seems there are various steps that might alleviate some at least of the problems. Some of the following emerged from on-site discussions with representatives of the Forestry Commission, the Woodland Trust, local conservation groups and interested local residents, local authority archaeological services, environmental consultancies, and others. These were further developed during and following the 2024 meeting.

Moss Valley woodlands, Derbyshire

Policy:

1) Changed status and designation of woodlands to reflect management history – a) *'Traditionally-Managed Ancient Woods'* b) *'Industrially-Managed Woods'*, and with preferential grant-aid for the former.

2) A more robust economic cost-benefit process to include **'No Net Heritage Loss'** and a costed **'Heritage Services'** element akin to 'ecosystem services' concepts.

The loss of the one-time 'Woodland Management Grants' is identified as problematic and the bureaucratic and complex forms of applications for current grant-aid are unhelpful. A simplified grant for managing an ancient, historic woodland in a sensitive and sympathetic way should be supported, and this needs to include the costs of specialist advice and project supervision. Current priorities for the Forestry Commission (and hence for landowners and woodland conservation bodies) are presently for bulk tree planting and not for site conservation *per se*. This can be seen in the allocation of employed staff by say the Woodland Trust, with priority given to planting 'new' woodland and not to conservation of irreplaceable 'ancient woods'.

Practice:

1) Effective site survey by specialist surveyors in woodland heritage features.

2) Site management plans adopted to include thorough heritage assessment to agreed standards.

3) Site survey recommendations adopted before work commences.

4) Recognition that ancient woods are cultural heritage landscapes and not merely a series of 'monuments' in an area otherwise devoid of interest – which appears to the stance taken by some Environmental Records Centres – leading to the loss of 'the bits in-between'.

5) Development of an accessible, comprehensive, authoritative handbook of woodland heritage.

6) Development of handy on-site guidance to understanding woodland heritage and avoiding unnecessary damage.

7) Support for the above by appropriate practitioner workshops.

8) Development of necessary support skills.

9) Development of enhanced grant aid for traditional woodland products and training of practitioners.

10) Adoption of robust heritage guidance within sustainable and environmentally-friendly forest product certification.

11) Re-connection with local communities better informed about what exactly an 'ancient wood' is and why they are irreplaceable.

Process:

The first step of all, is to accept that there is a problem with current woodland management. This involves the realignment of ancient woodland definition to fit traditional management and to alter grant support and certification accordingly. Without this recognition, there can be no effective, long-term solutions. Harking back to an earlier note about the comment from a senior Forestry Commission archaeologist some years ago, that *'even ancient woodland has to pay its way'*, my response was that they already do but we simply don't recognise it. Furthermore, current, publicly-funded woodland management reduces or even eliminates many of the services provided by effectively conserved and sustainably managed ancient woods. Compounding this devastating impact is a wall of silence in terms of any honesty with stakeholders and the public about what is happening and why. Worryingly too, the mainstream media has also been absolutely silent on these issues. But with woodland heritage, like the supermarket slogan, *'when its gone, its gone'*.

Meetings on damaged sites with stakeholders including Forestry Commission officers and their advisors, were in some ways positive but in other ways concerning. From some meetings there were very positive outcomes in principle, but nothing offered in the way of resources to bring about necessary changes like effective and accessible guidance for operatives. However, of genuine concern was the variance in opinion as to what constituted low level impacts of operations, what prior survey and assessment was acceptable, and the need to have in place agreed management plans (as described) and for these to be publicly consulted upon. It was considered acceptable to work on site with heavy vehicles, to do this with major constructed access roads, and to make deep incursions with ruts into the woodlands. All this was in sites with known but incompletely surveyed and assessed woodland archaeology, and with minimal support or guidance on site. The response from managers was in effect, '*this is how we do it*', and there is no other way. From a conservation viewpoint the impacts were highly damaging and unacceptable but from the forestry practitioner viewpoint, including a regionally senior advisor, they were fine. This was and is a serious problem.

There was a further issue that emerged through the consultations and discussions, and this related to the official processes of consultation, which for some schemes refers managers to the 'Environmental Records Centre' (or 'Sites & Monuments Records') of the relevant local authority and managed by badly understaffed archaeological officers. Having worked with many good professional archaeologists over many years, I am aware that many of them are not knowledgeable about woodlands or woodland management histories, and so this is a big problem. They recognise '**archaeology in the woods**' but not the '**archaeology of the woods**', and so this often remains unrecognised and unrecorded. Such oversight means that vital information may be overlooked, and this is compounded by most woodland heritage being unrecorded, and that which is, rarely being submitted to the system. Recording in the Records Centre at least ensures consultation on major projects such as site felling or development, but it is expected that the surveys and necessary recording will be undertaken by volunteers free of charge. Yet for an individual woodland, for this to be effective it might take many days of site-based survey and later analysis. Compounded by a lack of suitably experienced workers,

this means that most sites are unrecorded and thus fall through the net.

1980s photograph of medieval or early industrial charcoal hearth in Ecclesall Woods, Sheffield

A final problem is assessing the importance or the significance of recorded heritage or archaeological 'sites' in a wood, relates to an understanding of landscape and landscape history. The designation and recording system for archaeological features has evolved very much from a perspective of recorded, individual site, and whilst in more recent decades there evolved the idea of 'conservation plans' for heritage sites, there remains a legacy (sometimes) of a site being recorded and recognised as an isolated feature. Within a wood for example, charcoal hearths and whitecoal Q-pits might

126

be noted as a series of sites and these might be afforded a degree of protection. However, this opens up a fundamental problem of perception within the system and the process, and this was confirmed in discussions with local authority archaeologists on site. If a heritage feature such as an upstanding boundary bank with a ditch, a trackway, a building site or enclosure, or some form of platform like a charcoal hearth, is identified on site, then the cultural heritage is the entire landscape within which these features occur, not merely what is visible above ground. Current recording of woods, when it occurs at all, seems to be predominantly as a series of isolated point-finds, and furthermore, anciently-worked trees (some many centuries old), are almost always overlooked entirely. So, it seems that even the limited capacity for recording and consultation often falls at the first hurdle, and even when it does function, its influence is limited.

In conclusion, from long-term observations and case-studies, the two-day conference, site meetings, and associated consultations and discussions, it seems that there is a significant degree of agreement in terms of the issues and the need to reduce adverse impacts. However, there is a serious skills shortage relating to delivery of assessments, evaluations and guidance. Presently there is little available material published and few if any colleges or universities delivery the necessary training. There also remains a significant stumbling block in that key individuals differ in their assessments of what is acceptable damage to a site and for instance, what constitutes a low impact vehicle access.

A small, tracked machine on site and even this will obliterate bounders and earthworks

From a heritage standpoint, in known ancient woodland there should be very limited, if any, access by standard vehicles such as four-by-four offroad machines, tractors, lorries, or tracked vehicles. Where there is vehicular access, it should be restricted to already established roadways without the need for additional widening and minimal re-surfacing. Any management of trees needs to consider anciently-worked heritage trees, and should, wherever possible, be undertaken with chainsaws by hand. For cases of Disease Control Orders, the possibility of leaving deadwood standing or fallen on site should be considered – with benefits for biodiversity and habitat, floodwater retention, soil conservation, and carbon capture.

In calculating cost-benefit of interventions in ancient woodland, the fuller consideration of ecosystem services and cultural heritage services, presently not included, will affect assessments of financial viability. This will help lead to a more nuanced and balanced approach and the possibility of longer-term sustainability. The present 'smoke and mirrors' approaches are not fit for purpose and have little public accountability.

Industrial Q-pit or whitecoal kiln in Newfield Spring Wood, Sheffield

As discussed earlier, many of these problems and issues would be resolved by means of effective and adequately resourced site management plans, with not merely forestry, access, and ecological information and constraints considered, but a whole landscape approach to include cultural heritage, biocultural heritage (such as veteran trees), and archaeology both in the woods and of the woods. In the absence of such joined-up approaches then the losses and destruction will continue. Perhaps worst of all, because of the lack of agreed standards and protocols for survey, assessment, and monitoring, we have no effective means of even knowing what we have lost and what we are losing.

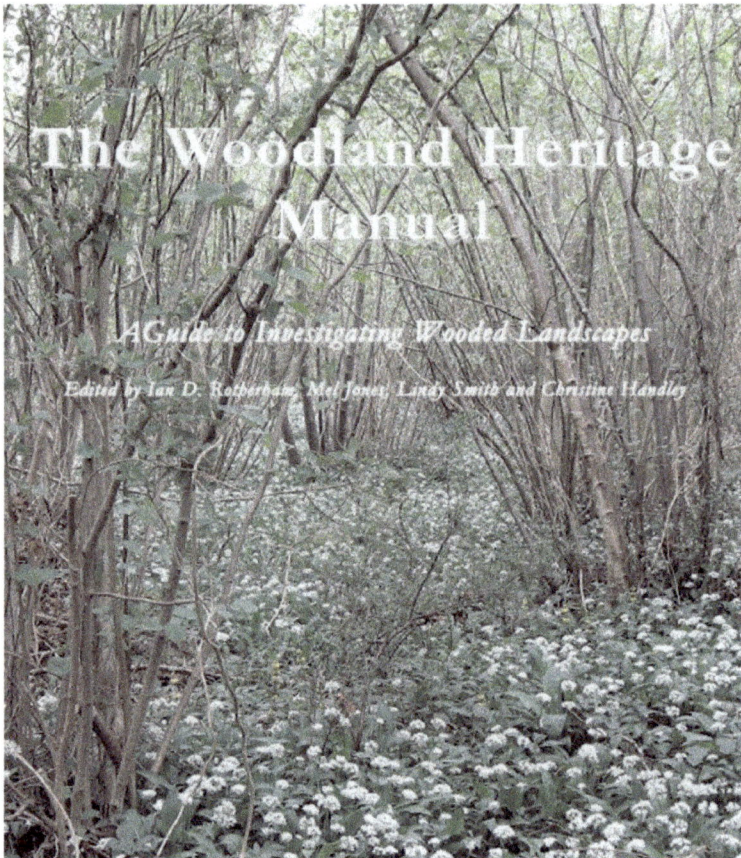

The manual provides guidance on site survey and assessment but needs to be updated

Summary guidance for site working to minimise adverse impacts

The '*Woodland Heritage Manual*' (Rotherham *et al.*, 2008) provides guidance on the evaluation of cultural heritage assets and why they should be protected. This approach accords with the assertions of Agnoletti *et al.* (2007). However, there needs to be a standard approach to archaeological evaluation, biocultural assets, and eco-cultural woodland heritage. Indeed, kite-marks for 'sustainable woodland management' (e.g., The UK Forestry Standard, and UKWAS) should in future include cultural heritage evaluation and conservation. The guidance outlined below moves some way towards this objective.

Identification of cultural heritage & archaeological features

For most woodland initially there may be little known about archaeology or biocultural heritage. In that case, the very minimum requirement is for a LiDAR (Light Detection and Ranging) overview followed by a walkover survey undertaken by someone experienced specifically in woodland archaeology and eco-cultural heritage. Inspection of early Ordnance Survey maps and estate plans if available helps to inform the process and to focus interpretation. Identification of field archaeology in woodland should help guide any future management and support the protection of significant cultural heritage. Initially the aim of such surveys is to raise awareness of features rather than create a detailed

131

historical timeline. Verification of some archaeological features may take time and resources but the objective at this stage is to minimise unnecessary damage and so generic identification may be acceptable.

Traditionally managed ancient woodland, Suffolk, 2007

Marking of features

The second stage of the survey process is to record site features by means of GPS (Global Positioning System) mapping, and to transfer the findings onto a GIS-based management map or plan. Prior to site management, areas or features of archaeological and cultural heritage sensitivity to be avoided should be marked on the ground using coloured flags or similar. The project operatives should be briefed in detail on these and if necessary given copies of the management maps with 'safe' access and exit routes marked and agreed.

Implementing management operations

Generally, traditional methods of management such as coppicing will have been less damaging than commercial forestry. However, in any current situations where machines are used then erosion, compaction, and destruction of extant and sub-surface features will occur and especially so when soil conditions are unfavourable. Dry, friable, sandy soils are particularly vulnerable, but damage can also be very bad in wet, muddy conditions. A summary of basic management guidelines for the cultural heritage of archaeological features is given in Table 1.

Table 1: Summary of Management Guidelines for Cultural Heritage of Archaeological Features
(Based on Rotherham, & Avison (1997) adapted from Bannister, 1996, but significantly expanded)
This Key Management Guidance is intended to minimise the disturbance to archaeological and other cultural and eco-cultural heritage sites, features, and resources.

• Ancient woodlands have archaeology **'in'** the wood (such as early industrial sites) and archaeology **'of'** the wood (such as tracks, boundaries, pits and platforms, and worked trees). • Both types of heritage must be identified, assessed, and carefully mapped. This must be by a suitably qualified and experienced specialist.	• Veteran and other 'worked' trees like coppices, stubs, clones, and pollards represent vulnerable living heritage. • Identify and map these trees and avoid disturbance. • This includes former (lapsed) coppices now present as singled, doubled, or triple-regrown stems.
• Record archaeological / heritage sites on management maps and inform workers, contractors, and	• Clear younger trees and shrub growth away from old pollards or coppices and where feasible recruit new pollards into the woodland structure. Maintain old

volunteers of their locations. • Prior to any woodland management, mark out the significant sites with posts or flags. • The consultants should be retained on a 'watching brief' basis.	pollards, stubs, clones, and coppice stools. • Areas of important ancient woodland vegetation and botanical indicator species (particularly rarities) should be surveyed, assessed, and mapped. Key locations should be avoided by operations on site.
• Avoid taking machinery over earthworks and buried / hidden sites – the heritage interest is not limited to the upstanding, visible features but is part of a historic or heritage landscape. • If this is unavoidable, cover the site with brash or other protective material and remove after use.	• Maintain, and if possible, restore any water features. Do not drain wet, mirey areas unless associated with damage to Public Rights of Way, in which case proceed with caution.
• Do not plough out or fence over archaeological sites. Do not plant up such sites. • If felling or clearing mature trees from ancient	• If coppice restoration is desired, then use dead-hedge fencing and restore traditional coppice

monuments for example, then minimise disturbance to the ground. • If it is necessary to control scrub growth, then do so by cutting or use of Forestry Commission approved herbicides.	management in shaws or coupes. • Where a site is heavily grazed, allow recruitment from seed bed. • If necessary to re-plant, use saplings grown from local seed-stock.
• Try to ensure that paths, bridleways, forestry access tracks, car parks, and wood processing areas are kept away from archaeological / heritage sites.	• If archaeological remains and finds are discovered while working, leave them where they are undisturbed and report them to the County Archaeologist / Environmental Records Centre. • Finds have greater significance when left in place. If removed they can become meaningless. • Refer to the 'Portable Antiquities Scheme' if needed. • Unless you have consent, do not use metal detectors on known archaeological sites.

• Within known ancient woods where there is identified or likely heritage such as banks and ditches, mounds, hearths and other platforms, trackways, earth-fast stones and worked stones, the use of large, heavy vehicles should be avoided at all cost. • This includes access off-road (i.e., forest tracks with vehicles such as 4x4 Land Rovers etc) often used for site access and transportation of personnel and equipment. This can be highly damaging when taken off the established forest tracks and if on historically flagged routes for example.	• Note that removal of trees with rot-holes and rot-pockets, if unavoidable, should not take place in the period from March to August (due to potential or likely presence of breeding birds) and without adequate assessment of bat roost potential (all year round). To carry out such operations is strictly prohibited by the Wildlife and Countryside Act 1981 (and later amendments) and may result in serious penalties.
• Maintain a photographic record of before, during, and post-operations.	•

• Survey, identify and map significant ancient woodland indicator plants.	• Note any areas sensitive to disturbance or disruption and mark clearly as 'no-go' zones.
Maintain existing routeways, and if necessary, restore any drainage channels after site working and reinstate any eroded paths with a suitable surfacing such as stone chippings (with appropriate alkalinity / acidity for the site) or wood-chip.	

Charcoal hearth in Ecclesall Woods, Sheffield, compromised by site footpath works around 1990s

Ultimately, if ancient woodlands are to be effectively conserved, as a matter of urgency, we need:

1) *Agreement on issues and on what is acceptable site practice.*
2) *Agreement on protocols for survey, assessment, evaluation, and reporting.*
3) *Necessary guidance and training as discussed.*
4) *Effective transparency on sites, processes, and on project finance.*
5) *Improved reporting and public accountability.*
6) *Funding for the necessary works.*

Final thoughts on the logic of contemporary woodland management

We need to consider why certain management operations are undertaken and what the perceived or expected outcomes might be. Having worked on historic woodlands, with woodland managers, foresters, and conservationists for over forty years, I have some pertinent observations.

Firstly, almost everyone working with woodlands and trees, be they volunteers or professionals, is passionate and positive about them. Indeed, this makes the current situation even more poignant as those working, in their minds, to safeguard woods are inadvertently destroying their unique 'ancient' character.

Secondly, it seems that quite often, management is undertaken without proper or effective survey and assessment, and in the absence of even the most basic agreed and approved management plans.

Thirdly, action research on woodland management projects further suggests that the reasons or purpose for active management are frequently at best obscure. Whilst organisations and projects may state 'nature conservation' as a primary objective, in practice this is often not the case. This may also apply to some **Biodiversity Net Gain** or damage offset schemes such as for instance, a suggestion by a developer's consultants to enhance local habitat in an ancient wood by plug-planting primrose, and rather bizarrely for a plant with a 'weed strategy', wood avens, both to compensate for habitat destruction associated with housing development. The wood avens proposal was just silly as it will arrive in due course by itself and carried on animal fur, and the primrose suggestion is simply inappropriate gardening and not conservation. This might be appropriate in a young plantation wood but not in ancient woodland.

Fourthly, action research on woodland management projects also indicates at best ignorance of the economics processes, and at worst deliberate misrepresentation. Many of the site-based works and case-studies described here do not make money and indeed they do not deliver much in the way of tangible products as outputs. Indeed, by and large, these project cost local authorities, conservation NGOs and other charities, and cash-strapped government agencies, along with other private landowners, many hundreds or thousands or even millions of pounds per annum. Orders are issued for instance for disease control, and the work must be done.

But step back and ask '**why**', and the response is a puzzled look. Usually, the reason given is to protect and safeguard the woods and trees and to stop the spread of disease. And yet the actions on the ground actually destroy most of the trees and turn ancient woods into post-industrial sites. Again, largely as an unnecessary sop to public relations, mass tree planting takes place to compensate for the damage done. This is wholly unnecessary since in a treed landscape, trees will self-set more quickly and for free, than can possibly be planted. The planting requires saplings, tree-stakes, tree-guards, further access to site and associated disturbance, and moreover it costs additional monies.

As I have argued (unsuccessfully) elsewhere, if we believe in the idea of ecosystem services provided by trees and woods, and with my suggestion of costed heritage services too, these woods already more than pay their way in 'public goods'. Yet the loss of these goods, the greatest value of the historic woods, through the damaging management, is not included in any economic assessment of work proposals. Public goods services include reduction of floodwaters, biodiversity, amenity and associated health and wellbeing, carbon capture, and soul conservation. Disruption of sites haemorrhages carbon, and causes soil erosion, ground compaction, destroys heritage and biodiversity, and exacerbates downstream flooding and water pollution. Public benefits in terms of health, wellbeing, and amenity, are also compromised. And of course, we are paying a lot of money for all of this. Rather worryingly too, in many cases, those experts proffering advice to undertake such works potentially benefit financial from the processes of implementation.

So why do we do this?

In terms of general management of ancient woodlands for conservation there is a perceived need to 'do something' rather than simply to be a custodian to care for a resource into the future and perhaps make sure access for instance, is effectively managed. For disease control and issues such as invasive species management, the drivers are usually what it says on the tin. However, the heavily destructive, machine-led approaches tend, in the long-term, to exacerbate problems and issues, and in the case of disease controls, there is little evidence that they work. Trees are felled and removed from site to protect the woods, but in so doing, the works destroy the woods anyway and generally fail to stop the spread of the disease. In all likelihood, the stress and disturbance caused by site work almost certainly makes the trees more vulnerable, and the felling removes potentially resistant trees from the population too.

If it is deemed necessary to fell trees in this way, then in ancient woods a combination of felling by chainsaw and, away from footpaths, ring-barking, are low-cost and far less damaging. Felled wood and timber can be left on-site to rebuild depleted soils and to sequester atmospheric carbon. Yet we feel the timber and then extract it to sell, in a process that loses money, but in order to pay for the works and both extraction and haulage. And yet it is often the latter, the extraction and haulage, which cause the irretrievable loss of heritage and ancient woodland character. This really makes little or no sense.

Lapsed coppice stool, Monk Wood, Derbyshire

1990s photograph of a Q-pit in Ecclesall Woods, Sheffield

1990s photograph of stone-revetted charcoal hearth, Moss Valley, Derbyshire

Chapter 6: A New World Perspective

My personal experience is of a countryside inhabited by people for many thousands of years and where the footprint of humanity is deeply embedded. Indeed, Britain has few areas which can generally described as 'old-growth' but the greater medieval deer-parks, the Scottish pinewoods, and maybe some former wooded common, 'shadow wood', has a resonance with this character. My 'ancient woods' have been managed by human communities for at least several centuries and often much longer, and this situation applies throughout much of Europe too. The problems I describe are experienced more widely but they vary with national histories, environmental conditions, and population densities. However, I did wonder about whether my concerns might cross the Atlantic to the so-called 'New World' and the Old-Growth / New-Growth forests of North America, and the answer was in a short volume called '*Nature's Temples – A Natural History of Old-Growth Forests*', by Joan Maloof. With her kind permission, I have extracted and summarised some of her notes.

On pages 2 and 3 Maloof writes about the structure and dynamics of old-growth. She notes how some trees can achieve their maximum natural lifespan and great size, and even where logging took place, remarkable specimens survive in wet areas or remote, rocky cliffs and outcrops where the felling didn't reach. This is reminiscent of the great lime trees that Donald Pigott mapped high above Coniston Water in the English Lake District, some being estimated at 2,000 to 3,000 years old. Similarly, great 'medusoid', multi-stemmed oaks hang on the cliffsides of crags in the Peak District or in Snowdonia for example.

'Although the trees in an old-growth forest are older and larger, fewer trees grow there than in a younger forest. One reason for this is that most of the light is captured by the tall canopy trees. Younger trees in the understorey must wait, almost in suspended state, for their turn in the spotlight when they might get the extra sunlight they need and finally make it to the canopy. If too many decades go by without the needed light, the younger trees may die. But if one of the ancients dies first, the large area that its canopy formerly occupied is now flooded with light, as if a massive sunroof had just been installed. In this gap even herbaceous plants that need full sun can thrive. Younger trees race to fill the canopy space. All nearby trees, even the oldest, shift their growth slowly in response to the change. From a godlike height the canopy no longer looks uniform. Like a tooth missing in a child's mouth, the fallen tree has created a gap that results in an uneven canopy. In terms of biodiversity, the gaps are as important as the ancient canopy. They allow sunlight in.'

This is a very neat description that easily transfers to an ancient woodland left for maybe two centuries unmanaged, with trees falling naturally, and regeneration cores of shrubs and trees, and herbaceous ground flora thriving in the gap. In a managed coppice wood, a similar process of light and shade occurs but in a shorter cycle, and it is these cycles and processes that traditional woodmanship sought to harness and use to produce underwood and timber.

'*Dead trees either remain standing or fall over. If they remain standing, they are called snags. Large snags, with their rotting wood and hollow spaces , create structural variation that can benefit many species, from the smallest insects the largest mammals. A fallen tree, likewise, creates structural diversity. The trunk as it rots helps to create new moisture-holding soil. It is a bonanza for soil-dwelling fungi that mine it for nutrients that they then pass along to the living trees. The woody debris is also important for forest-dwelling beetles and the organisms that feed on them. If the tree brought its roots along as it tipped over, the roots and the soil clinging to them create a mound that increases the structural diversity of the forest floor.*'

Again, this description applies equally well to the natural processes that will occur in a minimally-disturbed, mature, ancient wood in Britain, and as Maloof notes, the greater the tree the more topographic variation it creates. Certainly, in the past, it was these types of processes that nature conservation sought to harness and unleash. She goes on to describe how the bark varies between old trees and young ones, and that the mature forest has tall trees and ones twisted by age, again characteristics of more naturally-structured ancient woods. The crowns of the older trees may have short, angled limbs almost like antlers and forged in her words, by long periods of 'environmental assaults' reminiscent of the tortuous multi-stemmed trees on exposed, remate cliffs and crags in Britain.

On page 5, Maloof continues and quotes from Mary Byrd Davis in *Eastern Old-Growth Forests*, how '*we are between two forested worlds -the natural forest of pre-settlement North America and the recovered forest of the future ...... the earlier forested world is not dead. We are studying and struggling to preserve its living remnants*'. Even this has resonance with the ancient woodland ecologies that still cling on in less intensively managed places.

On page 26 and then page 29, Maloof notes some of the problems including accidental losses of trees such as when a student lodged tree corer in a bristlecone pine whilst trying the age it, and in order to retrieve the corer the tree, one of the rarest and oldest on the planet, was cut down. But less excusable is the argument put forwards by foresters at other sites is that the trees are old and '*if we don't cut the trees they are just going to fall down and die (or die and then fall down*). This is used as a threat to private forest owners to imply that unmanaged, the forest will simply 'collapse' and thus lose any monetary value. In fact, in old-growth forests annual fatality rates run at about 0.6 percent whereas in younger, cutover forests they were considerably higher at about 4.42 percent. In other words, the younger managed trees die at around seven times the rate of the older specimens. In Britain, the potential lifespan of a mature is frequently (and sometimes conveniently) under-estimated to justify felling, a situation apparently also observed in North America with trees capable of living for centuries being written off as being just about to die.

An argument often put forward is that a woodland or forest will simply recover after a period of clear-felling, and in North America this has been put to the test, as described on page 71 and subsequently. Interestingly Maloof focuses on herbaceous plants on the ground floor, which in Britain we might describe as ancient woodland indicator species. This is pertinent because whilst acknowledging the lack of comprehensive studies, it seems that those which have been done strongly suggest that following major disruption such as clear-cutting, the ground flora vegetation never fully recovers. In some cases, there is a short-term boom in species diversity where sun-loving and 'weed' species colonise into open, disturbed areas, and are quick to germinate. However, the perennial, shade-loving woodland and forest plants, often dependant on ants, molluscs, and small mammals or other fauna for seed dispersal, are permanently impaired by clear-cut logging. She quotes a study by Richard Brewer comparing ground floor vegetation in a forest stand in Michigan that was undisturbed for around 150 years since a felling period, and he was able to compare species richness in 1920, 1933, and 1974. This showed that whilst diversity changed over the period, the disturbed sites remained depauperate in comparison with the undisturbed ones and would likely remain so. Maloof then quotes studies in Lincolnshire in Britain, comparing ancient woods and recent woods, and the comment that, '*Claims that secondary woods will one day become as rich as ancient, presumed primary, woods seem unfounded*'.

Further studies in North America suggested the reasons for the differences and the long-term or permanent impacts. Research showed how old-growth forest had greater species-richness and vegetation cover on the forest floor. It appeared to be that the clear-cutting damaged the vegetation which then never fully recovered. A part of the explanation was direct damage of vehicles on the ground flora plants, but additionally, when clear-cutting removes the tree canopy, the nutrients vital to the ecosystem functioning at the forest floor are lost. In normal circumstances, with the aid of fungi, microarthropods, and earthworms, these essential nutrients are returned to the forest floor ecosystem when old trees die or major branches break and fall, and feed into the herbaceous layer. When the canopy is opened up, increased temperatures at ground level occur as sunlight is now direct and unimpeded, and this too affects shade-loving plants. Furthermore, resulting drought conditions due to altered microclimate may kill more sensitive plants. Some herbaceous plants, and indeed many so-called indicator species in British woods, do benefit from short-term bursts of light when a great tree falls naturally and is left. As explained by the late Oliver Rackham at one of the conferences I organised, this 'boom-bust' of light and shade is at the core of ground flora response to both natural treefall and coppicing cycles in traditionally managed ancient woods. Many indicators can grow and survive in dense shade and humidity but flower and set seed when a short-term gap opens. If the canopy gap persists then light-and drought-tolerant species such as competitive herbs and shrubs take over and the ancient woodland plants struggle. Indeed, this has been identified as driver of the processes of displacement of native, woodland plant populations in North America following disruption. The original old-growth plants can be squeezed out and prevented from re-establishment by competitive, invasive species introduced perhaps the forestry operations or else simply encouraged by the changed conditions. Furthermore, as in some British ancient woodlands, the characteristic ground flora species are in some cases dispersed by ants, and these may be removed or drastically reduced by clear-cutting operations. For many of these plants if their seeds do find a suitable regeneration niche in the disrupted forest floor, they may sometimes require a mycorrhizal fungus to establish And then take a long time to reach sexual maturity for seed production. This is the case in the studied North American sites and might hold true in Britain too. Whilst some species grow and spread quite

quickly once established, others such as wood anemone
(*Anemone nemorosa*) in Britain, spread vegetatively but
this can be slow, and in some cases under two
centimetres per annum. The most significant and
characteristic ground floor herbs of ancient woods of
old-growth forest, are what is called the 'vernal' or spring
flora, the flowers that grow, flower, and set seed before
the canopy closes in deciduous woodland and also
before the late summer drought induced by high
temperatures and great trees taking ground water as
transpiration. North American researchers have shown
that the '*low to non-existent recovery rates observed for
vernal forest herbs suggest that even a landscape of
hypothetically restored, old, secondary forest may not
serve to conserve and restore vernal-herb populations*'.
Other research found similar trends in abundance and
biodiversity for trees and shrubs of old-growth forests.

With old-growth sites now so reduced in North America,
steps have been taken to develop management
techniques to generate old-growth characteristics in
new-growth sites. This is somewhat analogous to work
pioneered in Britain by members of the Ancient Tree
Forum for veteran trees especially in wood-pastures, and
work we did in ancient woods in Sheffield back in the
1980s and 1990s, and which I am currently reviewing.
This selectively topped mature, exotic beech-trees to
leave standing monoliths and scatterings of dead limbs
and brash on the ground. Herbaceous plants, shrubs,
and tree regeneration cores quickly re-established under

the broken in canopy. A more detailed analysis in required to see how these sites acquire or not, the characteristics of ancient woods. The American research also sounds a note of caution that disturbance may trigger invasion by competitive, catholic plants and the expense of the old forest or old woodland flora, with seeds brought in on workers' boots, on machines, or windblown. The balance of more or less intervention management is to be debated and there is no definitive wrong or right answer.

On page 79 of Maloof's account, she raises an important matter of perception which I think applies to woodlands in Britain equally to forests in North America. She notes how walking through a local eighty-year-old forest close to home, with tall trees and verdant, woodland vegetation, all may seem well to the casual observer. The point being made that most people don't notice what they are missing and make the false assumption that this is ancient woodland or old-growth forest. A clear-cut forest or wood that seems to be recovering at least on the scale of our human lifetime, and it suggests that the original vegetation has been restored. There is even some research which supports such an assumption, but on closer examination this is based on baseline study plots which themselves are only a hundred to a hundred-and-fifty years post-disturbance. This generates the phenomenon discussed by Frans Vera for example in his expositions on European primaeval landscapes, of the 'shifting baseline syndrome'. Essentially most individuals have never experienced high quality, old-growth forest and ancient woodland firsthand, and therefore they don't know what to expect or what it looks and feels like. The 'extinction of experience' as it has been termed, means that we can't miss what we don't know. This may even be at the heart of my concerns about current levels of damage and destruction of ancient woodlands in Britain, because mostly we don't even know what it is that we are losing and, in many cases, have already lost.

Maloof closes with thoughts on possible futures, and I suggest you read the book. However, there is a salutary note on what is now left. She describes how '*our managed woodlands are a mere shadow of what once grew*', and whilst our British ancient woods are not directly comparable to the North American old-growth forest, the idea of perception and loss apply. Without effective baselines, people, even professionals in the field may assume and come to accept that degraded sites are the norm. The closest situation to the North American old-growth might have been somewhere like the once extensive royal forests of England, such as the medieval Sherwood Forest close to where I live. In the 1600s, the site boasted over forty thousand great forest oaks where today we have fewer than a thousand and many of those are dead. In the case of our ancient woods, managed by traditional woodmanship for around a thousand years, they have been affected and changed by long-term eco-cultural interactions. However, in most cases they avoided the massive disruption generated by

154

modern mechanised petrochemically-subsided management, and both their ecology and their heritage reflect this. A final comment is on the North American experience since the great old-growth forests were not uninhabited but were use d by North American First Nation peoples. Much of the evidence, the archaeology and heritage resulting from long-term habitation, sometimes over thousands of years, will have been erased and eroded by the same processes as now happen here in Britain. And again, like the biodiversity, we simply don't know what has been lost.

And finally, a postscript

A recent discussion with Paul Ardron and Jan Turner, two woodland enthusiasts based in Sheffield, highlighted for me the issue of knowledge and perception. Knowing of my passion for ancient willows and multi-stemmed sprawling giants, they brought me the image below photographed at Breney Common in Cornwall. This is a part of the Cornwall Wildlife Trust's Helman Tor Nature Reserve. What a magnificent tree and almost certainly centuries old sprawling as it does in every direction from a central point. There are similar specimens managed by the National Trust at sites like Penrose and Loe Bar.

So, imagine their horror when they returned to the site to find a footpath cut through the old veteran. Surely, the priority on a nature reserve must be conservation of nature and heritage, and this tree fulfils both criteria. If this had been a 500-year-old oak-tree I do not think this sort of damage would have happened. I am sure the conservation workers did not intentionally damage the heritage, but the problem is that they failed to recognise it. Therein lies a moral from much of this (hopefully) salutary account.

Ancient willow at Breney Common Nature Reserve – destroyed Photographs by Dr Paul Ardron

References & Bibliography:

Anon. (2014) *Practice Guide. Design techniques for forest management planning*. Forestry Commission, Edinburgh.

Anon. (2017a) *The UK Forestry Standard. The government's approach to sustainable forestry*. Forestry Commission, Edinburgh.

Anon. (2017b) *Socio-Economic Factors Influencing Coppice Management in Europe*. EuroCoppice Working Group 5, COST Action FP1301 EuroCoppice, Albert Ludwig University, Freiburg.

Anon. (2018a) *Practical guidance Module 2. Ancient woodland restoration: Survey and assessment of ancient woodland sites*. Woodland Trust, Grantham.

Anon. (2018b) *Practical guidance Module 3. Ancient woodland restoration. Phase 1: halting further decline*. Woodland Trust, Grantham.

Anon. (2018c) *UKWAS. UK Woodland Assurance Standard*. UKWAS Support Unit, Edinburgh.

Anon. (2018d) Nor Wood, Cook Spring & Owler Car Management Plan 2018-2023. The Woodland Trust, Grantham.

Anon. (2019) *Practical guidance Module 4. Ancient woodland restoration: Phase 2: recovery of the wider ecosystem*. Woodland Trust, Grantham.

Anon. (2020a) *Practical guidance Module 1. Ancient woodland restoration: An introductory guide to the principles of restoration management*. Woodland Trust, Grantham.

Anon. (2020b) *Practical guidance Module 5. Ancient woodland restoration Phase three: maximising ecological integrity*. Woodland Trust, Grantham.

Anon. (2023) *The UK Forestry Standard. The government's approach to sustainable forest management*. Forest Research, Farnham.

Bannister, N.R. (1996) *Woodland Archaeology in Surrey: Its Recognition and Management*. Surrey County Planning Department, Kingston-upon-Thames.

Barton, J., & Rogerson, M. (2017) The importance of greenspace for mental health. *BJPSYCH INTERNATIONAL*, **14** (4), 79-81.

Beresford, M. (2012) Earthwork Surveys and Test Pit Analysis at Whitwell Woods, Derbyshire. MB Archaeology, Unpublished technical report.

Bird, W., & van den Bosch, M. (2018) *Oxford Textbook of Nature & Public Health*. Oxford University Press, Oxford.

Çolak, A.H., Kirca, S., & Rotherham, I.D. (eds) (2023) *Ancient Woods, Trees and Forests: Ecology, History and Management*. Pelagic Publishing, Exeter.

Crow, P. (2003) *Managing the historic environment in woodland: the vital role of research*. Forest Research Annual Report and Accounts 2002–2003, Forest Research, Forestry Commission, Farnham, Surrey, 46-55.

Crow, P. (2004) *Trees and Forestry on Archaeological sites in the UK: A review document*. Forest Research, Forestry Commission, Farnham, Surrey.

Doar, C. (2016) *Management Plan for Moss Valley Woodlands Nature Reserve April 2016 – March 2021*. Sheffield and Rotherham Wildlife Trust, Sheffield.

Doar, C., & Willison, A. (2015) *Management Plan for Greno Woods Nature Reserve April 2015 – March 2022*. Sheffield and Rotherham Wildlife Trust, Sheffield.

Douglas, I. (2005) Urban greenspace and mental health. For UK MAB Urban Forum.
https://urbanecologyforum.org.uk/documents/papers/ukmabgrnspcepap2.pdf

Edwards, D., Elliott, A., Hislop, M., Martin, S., Morris, J., O'Brien, L., Peace, A., Sarajevs, V., Serrand, M., & Valatin, G. (2009) *A valuation of the economic and social contribution of Forestry for People in Scotland*. Research Report for Forestry Commission Scotland by Forest Research, Edinburgh.

Forestry Commission & Natural England (2015) *Ancient Woodland and Veteran Trees: Assessment Guide to potential impacts in relation to planning decisions*. Available at: www.forestry.gov.uk/pdf/150330AWAssessmentGuide2. pdf/$FILE/150330AWAssessmentGuide2pdf

Jones, M. (2009) *Sheffield's Woodland Heritage*. Fourth Edition. Wildtrack Publishing, Sheffield.

Jones, M. & Rotherham, I.D. (2012) Managing urban ancient woodlands: a case study of Bowden Housteads Wood, Sheffield. *Arboricultural Journal*, **34** (3), 215-233.

Li, Q. (2018) *Forest Bathing. How trees can help you find health and happiness*. Viking, Penguin Random House, New York.

Kirby, K. (2020) *Woodland Flowers*. Colourful past, uncertain future. Bloomsbury Wildlife, London.

Maloof, J. (2023) *Nature's Temples. A Natural History of Old-Growth Forests*. Princeton University Press, Princeton and Oxford.

Morris, J.K. (undated) *Woodland Archaeology in London*. Published by the Forestry
Commission and English Heritage, with help from City of London Corporation and the Museum of London.

Nisbet, T. (2025) *UK Forestry Standard Practice Guide Second edition. Managing forest operations to protect the water environment*. Forestry Commission, Edinburgh.

Peterken, G.F. (1981) *Woodland Conservation and Management*. Chapman and Hall, London.

Peterken, G. (2023a) *Ancient Woodland in concept and practice*. Chapter 1, in: Çolak, A.H., Kirca, S., & Rotherham, I.D. (eds) (2023) *Ancient Woods, Trees and Forests: Ecology, History and Management*. Pelagic Publishing, Exeter, 1-14.

Peterken, G. (2023b) *Concepts of Ancient Woodland*. Chapter 1, in: Rotherham, I.D., & Moody, J.A. (eds) 2024. *Countryside History. The Life and Legacy of Oliver Rackham*. Pelagic Publishing, London, 17-31.

Rackham, O. (1976) *Trees and Woodland in the British Landscape*. J.M. Dent & Sons Ltd, London.

Rackham, O. (1980) *Ancient Woodland: its history, vegetation and uses in England*. Edward Arnold, London.

Rackham, O. (1986) *The History of the Countryside*. Dent, London.

Rackham, O. (1989) *The Last Forest: Story of Hatfield Forest*. J.M. Dent & Sons Ltd, London.

Rackham, O. (2006) *Woodlands*. HarperCollins New Naturalist No. 100, London.

Rackham, O. (2023) *Archaeology of trees, woodland and wood-pasture*. Chapter 3, in: Çolak, A.H., Kirca, S., & Rotherham, I.D. (eds) (2023) *Ancient Woods, Trees and Forests: Ecology, History and Management*. Pelagic Publishing, Exeter, 31-71.

Rotherham, I.D. (2011) *A Landscape History Approach to the Assessment of Ancient Woodlands*. In: Wallace, E.B. (ed.) *Woodlands: Ecology, Management and Conservation*. Nova Science Publishers Inc., USA, 161-184.

Rotherham, I.D. (2012) *Traditional Woodland Management: the Implications of Cultural Severance and Knowledge Loss*. In: Rotherham, I.D., Jones, M. & Handley, C. (eds) (2012) *Working & Walking in the*

Footsteps of Ghosts. Volume 1: The Wooded Landscape. Wildtrack Publishing, Sheffield, 223-264.

Rotherham, I.D. (2013) *Ancient Woodland: History, Industry and Crafts*. Shire Publications, Oxford.

Rotherham, I.D. (2015a) Bio-Cultural Heritage & Biodiversity - emerging paradigms in conservation and planning. *Biodiversity & Conservation*, **24**, 3405-3429.

Rotherham, I.D. (2015b) *The Rise and Fall of Countryside Management*. Routledge, London

Rotherham I.D. (2017) *Shadow Woods: A Search for Lost Landscapes*. Wildtrack Publishing, Sheffield.

Rotherham, I.D. (2021) *Forest & Wood as Historic Archives of People, Place & Past*. In: Woitsch, J. (ed.) *European Forests – Our Cultural Heritage*. Nová tiskárna Pelhřimov & Institute of Ethnology of the Czech Academy of Sciences, Pelhřimov, Prague 2021, 11-28.

Rotherham, I.D. (2021) Challenges for the restoration of cultural values in UK woodlands. *Forest Ecology and Management*.
https://doi.org/10.1016/j.foreco.2021.119756

Rotherham, I.D. (2022) *Ancient trees and botanical indicators as evidence for change and continuity in landscape evolution*. In: G. Decocq (ed.) *Historical*

Ecology. Learning from the past to understand the present and forecast the future of ecosystems. ISTE, Wiley, New York, 123-134.

Rotherham, I.D. (2023) *The cultural heritage of woods and forests*. In: Çolak, A.H., Kirca, S., & Rotherham, I.D. (eds) (2023) *Ancient Woods, Trees and Forests: Ecology, History and Management*. Pelagic Publishing, Exeter, 15-30.

Rotherham, I.D. (2023) *Worked trees and ecological indicators in wooded landscapes*. In: Çolak, A.H., Kirca, S., & Rotherham, I.D. (eds) (2023) *Ancient Woods, Trees and Forests: Ecology, History and Management*. Pelagic Publishing, Exeter, 108-123.

Rotherham, I.D. (ed.) (2024a) *Woodlands: Ecology, Management and Threats*. Nova Science Publishers, New York, pp358.

Rotherham, I.D. (2024b) *Issues and problems for the conservation of heritage and archaeology in ancient woods*. Chapter 1. In: Rotherham, I.D. (ed.) (2024) *Woodlands: Ecology, Management and Threats*. Nova Science Publishers, New York, 1-33.

Rotherham, I.D. (2024c) *Evidencing change and continuity in woodland landscapes*. Chapter 7. In: Rotherham, I.D. (ed.) (2024) *Woodlands: Ecology,*

Management and Threats. Nova Science Publishers, New York, 153-172.

Rotherham, I.D. (2024d) *Historical woodland ecology: through the lens of ancient trees and botanical indicators*. Chapter 10. In: Rotherham, I.D. (ed.) (2024) *Woodlands: Ecology, Management and Threats*. Nova Science Publishers, New York, 209-233.

Rotherham, I.D. (2024e) *A case-study approach to reconstructing evidence for relict ancient woodlands from ecological indicators and archival sources*. Chapter 15. In: Rotherham, I.D. (ed.) (2024) *Woodlands: Ecology, Management and Threats*. Nova Science Publishers, New York, 301-329.

Rotherham I.D. (2024f) Comment: The new 'Locust Years' of ancient-woodland destruction. *British Wildlife*, **35** (4), 244-250.

Rotherham, I.D. (2024g) How modern management erases 'Ancient Woods'. *ECOS*, **45** (3), https://www.ecos.org.uk/ecos-45-3-how-modern-management-erases-ancient-woods/.

Rotherham, I.D. & Ardron, P.A. (2006) The Archaeology of Woodland Landscapes: Issues for Managers based on the Case-study of Sheffield, England and four thousand years of human impact. *Arboricultural Journal*, **29** (4), 229-243.

Rotherham, I.D., & Avison, C. (1997) Owler Car Wood: a report of its historic landscape features and proposed management. Technical report, Sheffield Centre for Ecology and Environmental Management, Sheffield.

Rotherham, I.D., & Avison, C. (1998) *Sustainable Woodlands for people and Nature? The relevance of landscape history to a vision of forest management*. In: *Woodland in the Landscape: Past and Future Perspectives*. Atherden, M.A. & Butlin, R.A. (eds). The proceedings of the one-day conference at the University College of Ripon and York St John, York, UK. 194-199.

Rotherham, I.D., & Handley, C. (eds) (2020) *Investigating Tree Archaeology. History and Technology of Woodland Management and Product Use*. Wildtrack Publishing, Sheffield.

Rotherham, I.D., & Jones, M. (2000) *The Impact of Economic, Social and Political Factors on the Ecology of Small English Woodlands: a Case Study of the Ancient Woods in South Yorkshire, England*. In: Forest History: International Studies in Socio-economic and Forest ecosystem change. Agnoletti, M. & Anderson, S. (eds), CAB International, Wallingford, Oxford, 397-410.

Rotherham, I.D., & Jones, M. (2011) Management issues in urban ancient woodlands; a case study of Bowden

Housteads Wood, Sheffield. *Aspects of Applied Biology*, **108**, 113-121.

Rotherham, I.D., Jones, M., Smith, L., & Handley, C. (eds) (2008) *The Woodland Heritage Manual: A Guide to Investigating Wooded Landscapes*. Wildtrack Publishing, Sheffield.

Rotherham, I.D., & Moody, J.A. (eds) (2024) *Countryside History. The Life and Legacy of Oliver Rackham*. Pelagic Publishing, London.

Sansum, P., & Bannister, N.R. (2018) *A handbook for updating the Ancient Woodland Inventory for England*. Natural England Commissioned Report NECR248, Natural England, Peterborough.

Saraev, V., O'Brien, E., Valatin, G., & Bursnell, M. (2021) *Valuing the mental health benefits of woodlands*. Research Report, Forest Research, Edinburgh.

Ulrich, R.S., Simons, R.F., Losito, B.D., Fiorito, E., Miles, M.A., & Zelson, M. (1991) Stress recovery during exposure to natural and urban environments. *Journal of Environmental Psychology*, **11**, 201-230.

Willis, K. (2024) *Good Nature. The New Science of How Nature Improves Our Health*. Bloomsbury Publishing, London.

Zeffertt, T. (1994) Whitwell Wood Archaeological Survey. (Unpublished).

https://www.gov.uk/government/publications/historic-environment-guidance-for-forestry-in-england/historic-environment-guidance-for-forestry-in-england (accessed January 2025)

https://www.forestresearch.gov.uk/tools-and-resources/fthr/historic-environment-resources/woodland-and-archaeology/ (accessed January 2025)

Author biography:

Ian Rotherham is Emeritus Professor, The Advanced Wellbeing Research Centre, Sheffield Hallam University, former Professor of Environmental Geography, Sheffield Hallam University and previously Principal City Ecologist, Sheffield City Council. He is an ecologist and environmental historian with a particular interest in the landscape history and conservation of woodlands and other countryside areas. He has written and published widely on these topics. He is contactable on ianrotherham36@gmail.com and there is more information on his website: www.ukeconet.org ; blog: www.ianswalkonthewildside.wordpress.com/, & on Twitter: @IanThewildside, & @ianthewildside.bsky.social

Moss Valley woodlands, Derbyshire

www.ingramcontent.com/pod-product-compliance
Lightning Source LLC
Chambersburg PA
CBHW040143270326
41928CB00023B/3333